T0065702

YOU
CAN'T
MAKE
THIS
STUFF
UP!

MARY ELLA

WESTBOW
PRESS®
A DIVISION OF THOMAS NELSON
& ZONDERVAN

This book is a work of non-fiction. Unless otherwise noted, the author and the publisher make no explicit guarantees as to the accuracy of the information contained in this book and in some cases, names of people and places have been altered to protect their privacy.

WestBow Press books may be ordered through booksellers or by contacting:

WestBow Press
A Division of Thomas Nelson & Zondervan
1663 Liberty Drive
Bloomington, IN 47403
www.westbowpress.com
844-714-3454

Because of the dynamic nature of the Internet, any web addresses or links contained in this book may have changed since publication and may no longer be valid. The views expressed in this work are solely those of the author and do not necessarily reflect the views of the publisher, and the publisher hereby disclaims any responsibility for them.

Any people depicted in stock imagery provided by Getty Images are models, and such images are being used for illustrative purposes only. Certain stock imagery © Getty Images.

ISBN: 978-1-6642-8298-8 (sc)
ISBN: 978-1-6642-8300-8 (hc)
ISBN: 978-1-6642-8299-5 (e)

Library of Congress Control Number: 2022920315

Print information available on the last page.

WestBow Press rev. date: 01/09/2023

Dedication

First and foremost, I want to dedicate this book to the lover of my soul, my best friend and savior, Jesus Christ. This is *our* book, and I love you so very much for walking me through all the many amazing moments in this life. Secondly, this book is dedicated to every person mentioned in the chapters. Thank you for being a vessel of God's *"You Can't Make This Stuff Up"* moments and for sharing them with me. I would also like to thank my Dad, Mom, and Poe for always making me aware of the Holy Spirit actively working in my life and constantly pursuing Jesus's heart. To my daughter, Piper, my son, Rorie, daughter-in-law, Jessica, and grandson, Camp, you are the lights of my life and examples of the love of Jesus to everyone you meet. I am so proud of you all and love you more than I can express. I also dedicate this book to the reader. It has taken me many years to get all these stories together and yet it was the most natural thing I've ever done. When God calls you to something, DO IT. Thank you for taking part in this adventure. I can't wait for you to have your own "You Can't Make This Stuff Up" moments........ are you ready?

Preface

⚜

She is clothed with strength and dignity, and she laughs without fear of the future.

(Proverbs 31:25 NLT)

Welcome! I'm so grateful that you picked this book up, and I'm sure you are curious about the title. What does *You Can't Make This Stuff Up* mean? Well, I will explain this most unique title and share how I have become a storyteller of what God can do. Isn't that what it's truly about—to know him better so that you can make him known to others?

I want to share with you a little bit about how this book was born. I have honestly known that at some point, I would write a book. I think it's something the Holy Spirit spoke to me about from a young age when I wrote my first short story at school. I loved the freedom to create a story just the way I wanted it; however, I put it off. I'm sure it was more about the resistance in the heavenlies than just me putting it off, but I ultimately chose to delay. But God! Don't you love that! When sweet Abba Father softly reminds you about a desire that he has for you and that you have put on the back burner? He tenderly takes you by the shoulders and steers you into "encounters", either with him, his Word, or other people.

Well, mine was other people, and it was super obvious. My daughter and I had just returned early from a mission school in Scotland and spent two weeks in quarantine because of COVID-19. During this time of isolation, the Lord brought two family members and a friend, whom I hadn't heard from in ages, into my life to speak words that I am sure they had no idea would allow the Holy Spirit to fan a flame that needed a good fanning. Their comments were almost identical and so very sincere. It went something like this: "I need you to live near me so I can be a better person, better Christian, and help me understand the Bible." This sent me on a quest in my spirit. I asked the Lord why these amazing women would feel this way. Because I'd been approached within two weeks with the same questions, what was my responsibility to this call?

Now let me stop any thoughts that I'm someone who has it all together, all the time. Nope! Nope! Nope! Just so you really get it… no way! However, I cried out to the Lord, saying the resounding, "Lord, you know me! You know how I constantly need to cry out to you over and over and over again. You know how confident I can be in something you've revealed to me, but then a couple of days later, I'll feel like I am doing everything wrong. Jesus, you know me."

Then at that moment, I felt Jesus say, *Yes, I do know you, and I've taught you things through all your tribulations. I've taught you how to keep your eyes on me, to catch it earlier and earlier, and to hand it to me when things start to spin out of control. You learned these things from me through other people of mine, and now it's your turn to tell others what you've discovered by walking with, trusting, and leaning on me and not yourself for understanding.*

Then it hit me like a load of bricks! I needed to compile a book of stories, which I had accumulated over the years. Stories that had encouraged and reassured me that the Lord was in control, even when it looked like the opposite. They were stories of God's faithfulness and his creative solutions, which I couldn't have ever come up with. There was a phrase that my precious and dear friend, Lois, and I had been using for three years to describe these stories. As soon as we sat down at the local coffee shop or our favorite restaurant—you know, the one with all the great atmosphere and the best chicken-salad sandwich EVER!—we would make eye contact, talk about what the Lord had done in our lives since our last meetup, and say, "You can't make this stuff up!" Then we would throw our heads back and laugh at all the Lord had done.

Since this started three years ago, this expression has spread everywhere we go. We began telling others about it, and they started using it. I even received a text yesterday from another friend. All it said was, "You can't make this stuff up!" I just had to laugh in joy at God's goodness.

I am starting to understand a little more about what the second part of Proverbs 31:25 means when it says, "She laughs without fear of the future" (NLT)

Wow! That's it! I finally understood. I have to put these stories of everyday occurrences down so that they continue to build others up. Then we, as Christ followers, will start to notice his perfect and creative strategies working in and through us. So that's where I am now with you, walking in the kingdom daily, learning to walk in his glory and his power. I trust that his plans for us are good and that he holds our future in his all-knowing and most-loving hands. I will be a storyteller!

Chapter 1

STORYTIME

One day Jesus told his disciples a story to show that they
should always pray and never give up.

(Luke 18:1 NLT)

I think I should hit a few of the high points from my life's journey, just so that you can get the gist of what shaped me to be the storyteller I am today.

You, like me, have stories that we tell our kids, our friends, and if you are like me or my absolutely precious mother, you tell everyone who glances your way. Why do we do it? Why do we feel the need to share these stories with others? I believe it's our innate way of leaving our mark on a generation or even sharing our ancestor's mark with a new generation.

When I was little, my mom would read me all kinds of stories—Bible stories, fairy tales, Mother Goose nursery rhymes, and so forth. If it wasn't a story she would read, it was a song story. My mom could read like no one else could. She read the characters as if she knew them personally and wanted me to feel as though they were surrounding me in my little bedroom. She was successful, from Jack jumping over the candlestick to the sweet little orange cat who was constantly being "scatted" away. My mom's storytelling ignited a love for hearing, reading, teaching, and eventually, acting out stories so that others would enjoy them as I did.

Of course like any good parent, my mother chose stories with moral or spiritual twists to them. Teaching me a lesson that one of them just might "remind" me of later when I was acting out. My dad didn't miss out on the fun either. He was a wonderful guitar player, and he loved playing for me and my little brother. Dad would turn a silly nursery rhyme into a jolly, musical folk song, which my brother and I would giggle and dance around the room to. Dad even threw in a few of his seventies' songs as well, and we would dance to those song stories just as wholeheartedly.

This wasn't the only avenue of stories and characters that affected my life. My mom's dad could weave some good ones. I remember sitting with a couple of my cousins around Papaw's big chair on the floor, as he would hold us in suspense to hear what he would come up with next. He was a big Irishman with red hair and a kind heart. He loved his family, and he loved telling stories that he had heard while growing up in Arkansas Riverbed country. His stories usually were about two brothers going off to war and one dying or a son going off to war and a mother mourning. Oh, would he have us all in tears! I remember us all exclaiming at the end, "Oh, Papaw! That's awful! That's so sad." He would almost be in tears himself, but then he would smile, say he had one more, and end on a sweet note of a story.

These memories and so many more shaped me into a storyteller. I come from a long line of them. My grandma wrote a small book about her life growing up and my mom and aunt wrote a book together as well. Along with telling stories, I also come from a long line of people who love the Lord Jesus. When you put the two together, you get some fun conversations. Over the years, I have found that there is nothing more satisfying than talking about my Jesus. He was the best storyteller, and his life was the greatest story ever told.

I encountered Jesus personally at the ripe old age of six. Yes, I said it—six years old. I can still remember those children's church multicolored wooden boxes, which were stacked up high to make bleacher-like seats, as I maneuvered my way down to seal the deal with my dear Jesus. I was blessed to be born into a family that had loved the Lord for generations, so I felt like I already knew him. But that Sunday morning, I decided that I wanted to go down to tell him how much I loved him and to give him all my life. You would think that from then on, it was smooth sailing, and I glided right into where I am today. Well, I hate to disappoint you, but life is life here on beautiful planet Earth, and I had many years ahead of me. Don't get me wrong; having Jesus on my side was my saving grace—quite literally—but we are fooled if we think we are exempt from being "pressed on every side." But just like the sweet scripture says,

> We are pressed on every side by troubles, but we are not crushed. We are perplexed, but not driven to despair.

We are hunted down but never abandoned by God. We get knocked down, but we are not destroyed. Through suffering, our bodies continue to share in the death of Jesus so that the life of Jesus may also be seen in our bodies.

(2 Corinthians 4:8–10 NLT)

Well, isn't that just refreshing and why in the world would we want to join this "set apart" group called Christ followers? If you give me a chance to set the stage for one of my stories, I hope to help you see why this life of loving Jesus is exactly the life to live and why none other matches.

My childhood was beautiful. I loved my family, immediate and extended. Jesus had stolen my heart in a way that I knew that I knew I was secure. I knew my precious Jesus friend and prayed about everything. However, as the years went by and life happened as it does happen, even to the most naive of us, who think, *"That stuff will never happen to me"* kind of people, I found myself having to deal with ups and downs. Family members and friends getting sick, dying, divorcing, and people living in ways that you grew up thinking were just bad. Then after a time, you think you are grown and look at life like nothing can touch me, and that's exactly where you find yourself, touched by the enemy. *What do you do now? How come God allowed that? Why can't I feel Jesus like I thought I would? Can I feel Jesus now? How?*

My goal for this book is to share with you my process of how the Lord is teaching me to release my troubles, negative feelings, beliefs that aren't in alignment with God's Word and character. Things that have kept me from walking in the freedom and joy that Jesus intended for me. I want to journey with you through a glimpse into the lives of people like you, who love Jesus, want to live for him and shine his love and presence everywhere they go. They are stories of real-life ups and downs and the way that we experience them and come out on the other side, able to see that the precious hand of our Heavenly Father has held us the entire way. We will go through things that we think will devastate us, trip us up, or possibly kill us, but in reality, they made us stronger, more resilient, and full of faith to face this life of living in the world but not of the world. It's the great exchange!

I want to point out that there are scripture verses at the beginning of each chapter that set the tone for that chapter and personal application questions at the end of most chapters that are meant for you to close your eyes, still your mind and spirit, and interact with Jesus. Ask the Holy Spirit to reveal where you are struggling and then wait on the Lord to show you how he wants to heal those areas. Ask the Lord what he wants you to believe instead of continuing to believe what you've been believing. Let's face it, none of us wants to keep feeling frustrated, depressed, anxious, lonely, shameful, fearful, or abandoned, and our loving Father doesn't want it either. He wants us to acknowledge the areas that the enemy is trying to keep us bound in and learn how to not only give these things to Jesus but also to ask what he wants us to believe in exchange— the great exchange. Our Father wants to give us a blessing to stand on, believe, and declare. He wants to give us new belief cycles and confidence that he is working all things together for our good.

Like the Bible tells us in Ephesians 6:10–13,

> Finally, be strong in the Lord and the strength of his might. Put on the whole armor of God, that you may be able to stand against the schemes of the devil. For we do not wrestle against flesh and blood, but against the rulers, against the authorities, against the cosmic powers over this present darkness, against the spiritual forces of evil in the heavenly places. Therefore take up the whole armor of God, that you may be able to withstand in the evil day, and having done all, to stand firm.
>
> (ESV)

Be aware that these negative feelings and battles we face are results of a war that is going on from the enemy, our flesh, or things that have been passed down through generations. Knowing and being aware of this is the beginning of freedom. When we know this, we can battle and win. It's a given: We will win, and we can walk in victory! So come with me, and let's see how these principles of warfare played out in my life and the lives of others.

I want to remind you that the questions at the end of most chapters are meant for you to close your eyes, still your mind and spirit, and interact with Jesus. This allows us to learn how to be still and know that he is God, anywhere, at any time, and on the fly! So let's dive in, enjoy some fun stories, and learn to interact even more with our Lord. Blessings, friend.

_____

_____

_____

_____

_____

Chapter 2

EXPLOSIONS

Forget the former things; do not dwell on the past. See, I am
doing a new thing! Now it springs up; do you not perceive it?
(Isaiah 43:18 NIV)

It was the Fourth of July, and in complete awe and wonder, my daughter, Piper, and I were standing in the backyard watching the fireworks that the neighbors were shooting off. These amateur firework show organizers had not only created an outstanding display order, but over the lovely community pond, each one went off without a hitch. The reflections were gorgeous. I was standing next to my baby girl, who was nineteen years old and my best friend to boot, and we were both entranced by the colors, which were contrasted by the night sky. Unfortunately, our trance ended when the last set went off. We were a little disappointed that it wasn't as powerful as the previous explosions had been. It was more like a fizzling out instead of a grand finale.

We turned and headed in while talking about how it was phenomenal, considering it was just a local display. We were almost at the door when a sudden, loud symphony of explosions caused us to jump and look up at the sky again. It was as if our neighbor was saying, "Gotcha!" He had let us believe that it had been over and done. Then just as we let our guard down, shrugged our shoulders, and thought, *Oh, well. After all, it was pretty good*, he sent off the best sequence of finale fireworks that I had ever seen. We stood there with our eyes as big as saucers and our mouths agape. We were speechless at the wonder of it all.

Isn't that how our Heavenly Father is with us? We are blessed and thankful for so much in our lives. We are in awe of everything that he has done. But then we get a mentality of not wanting to push our luck—as if that had anything to do with our Father's faithfulness to us. All of the sudden, he says, *Surprise! If you thought that was good, wait until you see this.*

So don't stop expecting from our Father in heaven. He loves to bless and keep us on this treasure hunt of knowing him more and him spoiling us. I love the verse in Joel 2:13–14, where Joel tells the people to return with all their hearts and not to give up. It says, "So rend your hearts and not your garments, and return to the LORD your God. For He is gracious and compassionate, slow to anger, abounding in loving devotion. And He relents from sending disaster. Who knows? He may turn and relent and leave a blessing behind Him" (NIV). Then in Isaiah 43:18, the Lord says, "Forget the former things; do not dwell on the past. See, I am doing a new thing! Now it springs up; do you not perceive it?" (NIV).

It is so amazing to me that Creator God, our Heavenly Father, tells us to forget about the past stuff, whether it's good, bad, or ugly, and not to dwell on it. It's like he is saying, *Sweetie, you have no idea what I am about to spring up into your life, and I want you to be aware of it. If you are dwelling on the past and the former things, you won't even be able to perceive the new things coming your way. So start expecting and watching for me to come through for you, again and again.* Wow! We have an amazing God who pleads with us to look deeper and beyond what we feel, see, smell, and hear with our spirits. He wants us to believe him for an awesome explosion in our lives!

- Ask the Holy Spirit to show you any place in your life where you feel like God has forgotten about you or your prayers.
- Now take a moment and write down one instance when he did show up.
- Thank him for showing up with explosions of blessings and thank the Lord for what he's going to do in your current situation that you are now praying about.

_____

_____

_____

_____

_____

Chapter 3

THE POTBELLY STOVE

For now we see but a faint reflection of riddles and mysteries[s] as though reflected in a mirror, but one day we will see face-to-face. My understanding is incomplete now, but one day I will understand everything, just as everything about me has been fully understood. Until then, there are three things that remain: faith, hope, and love—yet love surpasses them all. So above all else, let love be the beautiful prize for which you run.

(1 Corinthians 13:12–13 TPT)

My Aunt Martha recalled a story of when she had just finished gathering eggs from a fickle group of hens. She softly opened the heavy door of her cozy, little home, where she lived with two brothers, four sisters, a hardworking farmer-reverend father, and her charismatic, fun-loving, and full-of-Jesus momma. When she headed to where the stove was, she was a little taken back that her momma wasn't in the kitchen, where she had left her that morning. Then she heard the familiar exclamations of joy and amazement as Momma's head popped up from the well-worn space behind the potbellied stove, where momma was often found praying to her Lord. Martha looked quizzically at her mother. She knew that her precious momma was about to share whatever revelation that the Holy Spirit had whispered to her.

"Oh, Martha, the Lord just told me something marvelous. There I was behind the stove, this time praying for my friend to feel the call to ministry, and then the Holy Spirit said that it was me who had the call to ministry. Can you believe that? Here I thought he wanted me praying for my friend to hear the call, and it was I whom he was wooing." With laughter and admiration in her voice, my Aunt Martha said that her momma would clean with one hand while she held the Bible with the other and read it. Isn't that remarkable? You can't make this stuff up!

We often do what the Lord leads us to do, whether that is praying for someone, talking to a friend, or baking a casserole for a grieving widow. It is what I believe Paul is talking about in 1 Corinthians 13 when he says that we see a faint reflection, as though reflected in a mirror. Right now, we love our Lord with our whole hearts. Keeping our focal point on pleasing him and loving him is faith. We won't always understand what's going on in this crazy world, and it's so easy to move our eyes onto the chaos around us, but if we keep our faith and focus on Jesus, we will be protected from wasting our energy on things that don't matter or aren't Kingdom matters. We are a part of the Kingdom of God.

We are daughters and sons of the King of kings. He's our Father God. We wear a robe of royalty in the spirit realm. We can only see and walk in it by faith, believing that there is more and that we are only going to see and understand in part. If we have faith, hope, and love, we will fully understand everything, and our Father will be so very proud that we trusted him, even when we couldn't see the whole picture. That's what Martha's momma did. She prayed for her friend wholeheartedly because that's what she saw in that faint mirror. Then the Lord clarified a different purpose for her intercession. What if she hadn't gotten on her knees and prayed for her sister in the Lord? Would she have gotten clarity about her calling? We must go before our Lord with humility and vulnerability and listen to what his Spirit has to say.

Remember what Jesus said about the Holy Spirit to the disciples in John 16:13: "However, when He, the Spirit of truth, has come, He will guide you into all truth; for He will not speak on His own authority, but whatever He hears He will speak; and He will tell you things to come" (NKJ). Who is better to trust than the Spirit of the living God? He knows everything that the Father speaks, and he can reveal it to us personally when we stop, are still before the Lord, and listen to what he says about a thing. Thank you, Holy Spirit, for staying with us and imparting the words of the Father to us.

- ~ Take a minute and ask the Lord what or whom he wants you to intercede for today.

_____

_____

_____

_____

_____

Chapter 4

HAND-ME-DOWNS

But how can people call on him for help if they've not yet believed? And how can they believe in one they've not yet heard of? And how can they hear the message of life if there is no one there to proclaim it?

(Romans 10:14 TPT)

I was at my dear friend's house, spending the afternoon chatting, catching up on our kiddos and jobs, and talking about Jesus—of course. Isn't it amazing how you can't help but talk about the things you love and care about? Well, that is how my conversation weaved its way back to Jesus and all he has done in our lives on that day with my friend. We also talked about all the new things that he was doing in our lives and families. You know, like new scriptures we had read or something that we had heard in church that had jumped out and made us think more deeply.

So this was how the day was perking. Then my friend suggested that I stay for dinner. I didn't want the fellowship to stop either, so I eagerly agreed and offered to help cook. She said that she wanted me to taste her mother's potato soup recipe, which would ruin any other version I had ever had. She picked up the phone, dialed her mother's number, and after two rings, I could hear her mother's sweet voice on the other end. The conversation was hilarious. My friend asked for the priceless recipe, but her mother responded with, "Oh, Tammy, I don't have that recipe written down anywhere."

This caused my friend to respond, "Well, Mom, can you just tell me what you put in it?"

To which the sweet lady on the other end said, "Well, let me think here. Hmmm, you know, I can't think of it when I'm not fixing it. It's just second nature when I'm in the kitchen."

My friend told her mother not to worry about it., but then said something that shouldn't have been that big of a deal, but it hit my spirit deeply. My friend said, "Mom, how can I pass this on if you never tell me how you make it?"

It's so comical to me how the Lord gets you to sit up and listen. This was convicting to me as well, because I needed to write this book, but I had put it off for quite a while just because I didn't stop and do it. Then a deeper revelation developed in my mind. *Is this what Romans 10:14 is trying to declare across the gap of time, looking into eternity? Was Paul pleading with believers to share their stories and tell someone about what the Lord had done in their lives?* I know that my life, family, and friends are not the only ones who have stories that cause people to throw their heads back and belly laugh because the Lord did something so cool that made them say, "You can't make this stuff up!" These personal stories are what make Jesus real to people. They are stories of how our almighty God gets down in the plans and schedules of our day-to-day lives and pulls out the coolest twist of events.

I can't tell you how many times I have sat back, looked at where I am, and said, "You couldn't have told me that I would be here right now. Who would have thought it?" After a while of noticing his awesome maneuvering in my life and his going above and beyond what I would have ever thought, I started getting excited about what was next. When a situation arises, I say to my Father God, *Oh, I can't wait to see what you have up your sleeve. I know it's going to be good.* Tell others about the small and big things. Talk about the Lord doing things that knock your socks off or seem completely confusing but turn out alright in the middle or result in you being able to say, "God did it again!" because those are the things that build your faith and the faith of others. Start expecting him to surprise you and to work *everything* out for your good. At times, it might not be obvious that he is working, but he is. He said so in his Word, and he is not a man that he would lie. He is God. How will they know about him if we don't tell them?

~ What God story in your life or your family members' or friends' lives do you need to tell that brings glory and a testimony to all God is up to for our good?

_____

_____

_____

_____

_____

Chapter 5

GRANDPA'S HEALING

He [Moses] persisted in faith as if he had seen God who is unseen.

(Hebrews 11:27 TPT)

My grandfather on my dad's side was Thomas Love. He was such a man of God and larger than life to me. He was a pillar of faith in his community as well as in our family. As a barber, he was used to carrying on conversations with many different people's personalities. He used every opportunity. Whether while he was cutting someone's hair or talking with someone in line at the bank or post office, Grandpa Love would make sure that he let others know they were important and loved by Jesus. He would also tell stories of his life, where the good Lord had come through for him over and over again.

He was such a neat man. I loved going to visit him and my grandma. They would meet us at the door of their white farmhouse, which had sat and watched as it went from a lone house in a field to an entire city being built up around it. Their humble home saw children being born and growing up. It even went through a season of welcoming borders when the depression hit our nation back in the 1930s, and many families had to rent out rooms in their homes to boarders, along with many other money making options to help make ends meet. Needless to say, my grandparents went through a roller coaster of many decades and learned a great deal. They watched their amazing Lord work many miraculous signs and wonders in their lives, as well as in the lives of others.

My grandpa told one story that always made the hair stand up on the back of my neck, and part of what formed who I am today. Someone who knows that her God is good and confident that he can do the miraculous.

As I was praying about the verse that best fits my grandfather's story, I was torn between his favorite verse, which is Proverbs 3:5–6, "Trust in the Lord with all your heart. Lean not on your own understanding. In all your ways acknowledge him and he will direct your path" (NKJV) and Hebrews 11:27, "He persisted in faith as if he had seen God who is unseen." Ultimately, I decided they both fit my grandpa, but the Hebrews scripture was the one that best described the faith he had as a young boy, who had been born club footed in 1910 and had to be pushed to school for many years in a cart pulled by a goat.

Yes, that describes my Grandpa Love's faith. As I remember the story, Grandpa was about thirteen years old when a healing preacher came into their community and held nightly tent revivals. Many were being healed under the large canvas tent that hovered over the crowd, as the presence of God filled the atmosphere. One by one, people made their way to the altar and gave their lives to Jesus or raised a hand so that they could receive the prayer of faith and be healed. My grandfather heard of these miracles and told his father that if he would just take him to the tent meetings where the healing evangelist was praying, he knew that he would be healed. His father agreed, and off they went to the large tent in the middle of the field to connect their desperate son, who was filled with faith, to the healing power of God.

They arrived, and as the evangelist laid his hand on my grandfather, I remember him telling me that he just knew he was being healed. That was a little disturbing to me as a child because I asked, "being healed? you weren't immediately healed?" This is when my precious grandpa would place his shaky hand on my hand, squeeze it, and say, "I went back for seven nights, and every night, the Lord Almighty, with his healing power, would do a deeper and deeper work until I was walking. I never rode in that old goat cart again!" He was proud of the way that the Lord had healed his body. It was a huge part of his story, which he told to almost all of the customers who sat in the barber chair of T.F. Love. I never heard him say that the "process" was an issue. He was so thankful, and he knew that his God was good and faithful. This would establish a foundation that would carry him through hard times to come and give him rewarding moments that would encourage him to press on toward the goal.

- ~ What are you believing God for that might be in the process?
- ~ Take a moment to ask the Holy Spirit to encourage you to stay the course, knowing that God is faithful and able to accomplish everything that you are believing him for.

_____

_____

_____

_____

_____

Chapter 6

THE RELEASE

---†---

Elijah went before the people and said, "How long will you waver between two opinions? If the Lord is God, follow him; but if Baal is God, follow him.

(1 Kings 18:21 NLT)

There is nothing in the world like the feeling of an answered prayer. One you have warred over and released to the Lord. Trusting that he can and believing that he will do what he said he would do. This is exactly where I was as I drove the interstate from Arkansas to South Carolina, where I would spend the week before the wedding of my firstborn and only son, Rorie. But let me back up about ten-to-thirteen years prior to the telling of this story.

My son was born with a powerful anointing on his life. When he was about ten years old, his desire for everyone to love Jesus like he did, made him create what he called the "God Army", which was made up of his guy friends from around the neighborhood. They would dress up in army fatigues, paint their faces, and head to the woods and creek to run drills for battle while chanting their axioms from the Men of Honor camp that they attended every summer. He was determined to spread the good news of Jesus.

One evening, I went into his bedroom to pray with and say goodnight to him. He met me with his small red metal lockbox, which contained his most valued treasures and money that he had made working for his grandparents. I sat down on the edge of his bed. With serious determination, he said, "Mom, I need you to do something for me."

I responded, "OK, sweetie. What do you need?" He had pulled ten dollars out of his lockbox, handed them to me, and said, "Tonight, I called into KLOVE, the local Christian radio station, and pledged ten dollars a month. Can I give you the cash, and you pay for it?" My heart melted as I realized that my son loved Jesus so much that he wanted to share him with others. He loved people that much as well. I knew his heart was tender. How much this little boy was going to be used by the Lord resonated with me.

My son has a heart after God like King David's. Just like in King David's life, there is an enemy who wants to try everything that he possibly can to stop the promise of the called. My boy got hit very hard by the enemy when he was about twenty-one. All along, this momma and our family and friends prayed and fought until he came out of his time of running from his call. When he did, our Jesus was so sweet. He took him in his arms and brought him back, just like the prodigal son's father did. He ran down the road into his father's arms. He was totally accepted, forgiven, and set back on the path and in the family.

Going through that time was difficult. I was single after twenty-one years of marriage, and my son, who had always been a family guy and loved the Lord, was now turning his back on everything and everyone. My knee-jerk reaction was to plead with and remind him of all the things the Lord had done for him and our family. I even got to the point of taking scriptures to him, that would remind him of who he was in Christ and how deceived he was. He would nod, agree, and say, "Your right, Mom. I'm sorry. I'll change." However, he never did, and I became even more fearful.

One evening as I was on my knees praying for my sweet boy, I felt the Holy Spirit whisper clearly to me to stop and read Genesis 22, where God tells Abraham, *"Take your son, your only son, whom you love—Isaac—and go to the region of Moriah. Sacrifice him there as a burnt offering on a mountain I will show you."* After I read the entire chapter, I was reminded of Abraham's trust in the Lord, which made him able to obey the Lord when God gave him these strange instructions. I saw how faithful God was to Abraham when he spared his son, Isaac. Then the Lord showed me another layer that resonated with me from my head to my toes. He pointed out that not only was this a test of Abraham's faith but also a reminder to Abraham that God was his first love. Even though this precious son of promise was a gift of God to Abraham, Isaac was not to replace his love of God, which was first and foremost. I was starting to see that God wanted my heart completely as well. He was asking me to trust him with my whole heart and to lay my son on the altar. It wasn't only for me to learn to trust him no matter what it looked like in the physical, but also the way the Lord would get my son's heart wholly, completely, and with no compromise.

When that clicked in me, I wanted it. I wanted my son to know his God on his own and choose whom he would serve. I am reminded of what Elijah set before the people in 1 Kings 18:21, "Elijah went before the people and said, 'How long will you waver between two opinions? If the Lord is God, follow him; but if Baal is God, follow him'" (NIV). The people that Elijah was speaking to said nothing in response. They didn't know what they believed. I declared in Jesus' name that this would not be me or my family. *OK, Lord, I surrender my life and my son to you. Pursue each of us, let us both fall deeper in love with you, and help us to trust in you because of this experience. We are yours, and you are good!*

At first, time went by slowly after this release, but then I got better at turning things over to Jesus quicker and quicker. Yes, it was a long journey, and at the time, it felt like too much time was going by without talking to my son or knowing where he was, what he was doing, and whom he was with. I heard things every once in a while, and they weren't good. I knew that this was not my son's true identity.

Then one day about a year after it all had begun, I was driving by where he worked. I felt the Holy Spirit nudge me to find his truck, so I slowly weaved up and down the aisles of the parking lot. It was late at night, and I was by myself, but I found it. I got out, laid my hands on the vehicle, and declared, "In Jesus's name, I bind every demonic spirit trying to influence my son and say go to the foot of the cross now. Go to where Jesus would send you. My son is a child of God, and you have no authority over him. I plead the blood of Jesus over his truck and him. I ask that every time he gets in this truck, the power of the Holy Spirit will overshadow him and love him back to the Father." This began a routine that my daughter joined me in. We took anointing oil and prayed. Next, we found out where he lived, and we did the same thing there.

Later after he had returned, I asked him if he had known that we had prayed. He said that he didn't know in fact but that he knew in spirit. He said that he would tell his live-in girlfriend, "My mom's been praying here. I can sense it." One time, he said that he almost fell off the balcony but that he felt something push him back up. He exclaimed, "My mom and sister are praying angels around me!" So, mommas, if you have children running from Jesus, keep those prayers and declarations going. They do work, and they are effective in the pulling down of strongholds in our children's lives.

> The weapons we fight with are not the weapons of the world. On the contrary, they have divine power to demolish strongholds.
>
> (2 Corinthians 10:4 NIV)

Piper and I continued listening to the Holy Spirit's nudges and warred in prayer. We prayed in the Spirit on all occasions.

> And pray in the Spirit on all occasions with all kinds of prayers and requests. With this in mind, be alert and always keep on praying for all the Lord's people.
>
> (Ephesians 6:18 NIV)

It was amazing how the Lord brought people who truly had a burden for Rorie to pray with me. They were so encouraging, and I will never be able to thank them all on this side of eternity. The Lord also led me to videos, teachings, books, and preachers who spoke right to me regarding what I was going through. One in particular was Karen Wheaton. She is an amazing woman of God with a ministry out of Alabama. She went through a similar experience with one of her children and wrote about the journey and the way that the Lord walked her through it.

It had been about two years by then, and I was listening to Karen's audiobook *Watching the Road: Praying Your Prodigal Home* when she told of the time that the Lord said, *Say it out loud!* She started declaring that her daughter was back and that her marriage was healed. So I did the same thing. Karen wanted to declare it to everyone, but it was the middle of the night, and no one was around, so she decided to go to her car and "pretend" to call people, and say it out loud, over and over. I decided to do the same thing. I pretended to make phone calls and declared, "Rorie has returned to the Lord and his family. He has met and married a mighty woman of God, and they are serving Jesus together in ministry." I made the calls and even declared it to my daughter, niece, mom, friends, and family. I said, "It shall be so, in Jesus's name!"

Two months from the day that I started declaring it, I received a phone call from my son. He said, "Mom, I have to leave this life. It's not me. I have to get out. Will you help me?" Together with Jesus, we walked my son out of that life and into a time of healing and restoration. It was almost immediate. The turning around and desperate run into the Father's arms that my son did was just like the story that Jesus told about the prodigal son running into his father's arms. I rejoiced with him. Words truly can't express how my heart felt. His journey solidified his heart. He no longer walks between two lines. He follows Jesus with all his heart, on his own. My son was lost, but now he's home.

- My dear friend, I know it can feel like forever when we go through times that seem so very desperate, hopeless and like no matter what you say or do, nothing is going to change—in fact, it seems to get worse. Your situation may not be a child who has walked away from the Lord, but it could be another lost loved one or friend. You may know someone with a terminal illness, and it seems all hope is gone. Close your eyes right now and ask the Holy Spirit to give you a promise to stand on for this situation and declare over and over again. Then write down what he tells you below.
- Now Declare It! It can be a pretend phone call or out loud in your room or yard. Let the enemy know that you believe what the Lord has said about it and that you are ready to do war. It is finished!

_____

_____

_____

_____

_____

Chapter 7

STEPPING OUT
IN FAITH

Trust in the Lord and do good; dwell in the land and enjoy safe pasture. Take delight in the Lord, and he will give you the desires of your heart.

(Psalm 37:3–4 NIV)

A year and a half after Rorie had come back, his sister told him about the missions' program that she and I had been a part of in Scotland. She felt like he needed to go do the same program in California. She even made a powerpoint, which laid all the details out for him. Thank the Lord for a praying sibling that isn't afraid to stand in the gap. By this time, Rorie had gotten a good job, and he was doing well, but Piper felt in her spirit that he needed to step out in faith and go see what God had for him in ministry. We all knew that he had the amazing gift of loving people and teaching others about Jesus. At first, he wasn't sure what to think of quitting his job and selling his truck to pay for the school, but after praying and encouragement from his mother, sister, family, and friends, we were on our way to California.

As he walked onto the campus, I saw that little boy in his face again. He was a little scared of the unknown, but there was enough drive to push him forward and see what God had for him. After months of dedicated time with Jesus and others who had similar hearts, he was ready to go anywhere and do whatever Jesus wanted. I tell you what; this momma was praising God for his faithfulness to answer prayers and to the generations. To top it all off, by the end of his school time, he fell in love with a young woman who loved Jesus with all her heart as well. They both felt a call to serve the Lord and go into all the world.

That brings me back to where I began the last chapter: driving to South Carolina and praising the Lord for his faithfulness to us and his promises as I headed to my son's wedding. He was marrying the woman of God with the beautiful name Jessica that I had declared and believed for, since I was pregnant with him. God had been faithful to bring my son and her together. Their wedding was amazing. It was full of family and friends from all over the United States. It was such a sweet time of love and redemption.

It's been a year, and a lot has happened in this beautiful couple's life. They adopted a sweet baby boy, my first grandchild. It makes me think about the scripture verse that says, "But blessed is the man who trusts in the LORD, whose confidence is in him. He will be like a tree planted by the water that sends out its roots by the stream" (Jeremiah 17:7 NIV).

The Lord is so sweet when we walk with him. Not only does he answer prayers but he also gives us the desires of our hearts. He does things for us or gives us gifts and treasures that we don't even realize that we want. He knows us that deeply and cares about giving us good gifts.

_____

_____

_____

_____

_____

Chapter 8

DIVINE INTERVENTION

For a people shall dwell in Zion, in Jerusalem; you shall weep no more. He will surely be gracious to you at the sound of your cry. As soon as he hears it, he answers you. And though the Lord gives you the bread of adversity and the water of affliction, yet your Teacher will not hide himself anymore, but your eyes shall see your Teacher. And your ears shall hear a word behind you, saying, "This is the way, walk in it," when you turn to the right or when you turn to the left. Then you will defile your carved idols overlaid with silver and your gold-plated metal images. You will scatter them as unclean things. You will say to them, "Be gone!"

(Isaiah 30:19–22 ESV)

Piper and I were traveling through Northern California, on a journey of listening to the Holy Spirit. Lord, should we go to family, friends, a retreat center, or an Airbnb? What should we do, Lord? Where should we go, Lord? No audible voice declared where we were to head to or where we should stay, so we planned. Isn't that the way we often do things? We pushed forward to do what seemed the best fit, most logical, and least expensive, just to be real. We decided to head to a retreat center we had heard about. Even though we continued to plan and walk out what we thought was best, we were continually saying, "Holy Spirit, if this isn't your will, turn us where you want us to go. Lord, we only want what you want."

Now, when we put things truly in his hands, we had better be ready for him to do something, and better recognize it when he does. We had made dinner plans with a family member we hadn't seen in years before we headed out the next day for the retreat center. So there we sat at dinner with family members whom we didn't know well, and as usual, I felt the need to start the conversation. After a bit of talking back and forth, I noticed confused faces. They looked at us like we were aliens, as people sometimes do to southerners who are visiting Californians. The entire time, the Holy Spirit was dropping things in my spirit to talk about, and I wasn't sure why, but man, Jesus knew what to say.

The boyfriend of our family member is a corrections officer at a major maximum-security prison in California. He had been pretty quiet throughout dinner but seemed like a really nice guy. All of the sudden I thought of something that might draw him into the conversation. I shared about a time when my prison minister stepdad had me teach a Christmas morning service to 250 inmates at a high-level prison in Oklahoma. That immediately got his attention, and I saw his eyes light up. Wow! Who would have thought something that happened three years ago would capture the attention of the muscle-bound man with such a big heart? He became extremely engaged and as the conversation progressed, he shared with us that the area where the retreat center was located was not safe and that we needed to be careful. I tucked that away and went on to tell the group that they would be in our prayers and that we had had a wonderful evening.

As we lay down that evening, I continued to feel a nagging in my spirit. Again, I prayed, *Lord, lead us.* My daughter and I woke up the next morning and neither of us voiced any doubts about heading to the retreat center. We loaded our car, drove down the road to the closest Dutch Bros. Coffee stand, and sat in silence, which if you can imagine, is not the norm for me. My mind was spinning, and my heart was racing. How would I tell her that I now had a check about the place we were supposed to be heading to after we slipped out of the coffee line? I now had a check, but I didn't have a clue where we should go. I felt like it was getting to be a regular thought process as we traveled that new moment-by-moment Holy Spirit-led life.

As if on cue, she turned to me and said, "Mom, are you concerned about what they said regarding where we are going?"

I wasn't concerned because I knew that if it was where the Holy Spirit was leading, we would be in the safest place—His will—but I did believe it was another warning that maybe the Lord had other plans. I looked at my daughter and said, "Well, I don't feel peace in going."

To which she said, "Mom, let's park and pray!" We found a parking lot and scooted right in.

We prayed, "Lord, we know you have us on a journey and that we are in your sovereign hands. Where do you want us to go? What do you want us to do? Where … What … How … Etc … you know the drill."

We sat in silence, hoping we would get a grand vision or hear an audible voice, but instead, a still, soft voice whispered to my daughter. It said that we needed to write down the last thing we knew the Lord had told us to do. I immediately knew it was to finish this book, so Piper jotted that down on the list. Then instantly, a post from Instagram popped up. It was a word from a minister that we follow, named Jolynne Whitaker, and it said the following.

Prophetic Word

November 2, 2020
Given Online by Jolynne Whitaker

I heard the Lord say, you know you're called. You know what you heard Him say. You know what He told you to do. Glory to God!

Oh yes, you know it's your season and you sense your moment drawing near. Yet the details contain so many questions, and you just don't have all the answers. You don't have the resources or needed wisdom, for that matter. Well God sent me to declare that IRON SHARPENS IRON—advisors, and helpers are coming, in Jesus' name!

He said to tell somebody, THIS is indeed your ACCEPTABLE YEAR of the Lord—when God is going to give you beauty for ashes, the oil of joy for mourning, and a garment of praise for that old heaviness, for you shall be PLANTED and become a tree of righteousness before the Lord.

Hallelujah to Jesus!

TO THAT END, HELP is coming your way! HOLD ON, ASSISTANCE is coming, in Jesus' name!

I prophesy God is about to put your name on the heart of someone who can help you. He's going to drop your name in the spirit of someone who can ADVANCE you, FUND you, GUIDE you, even ACCELERATE and ADVISE you—IN JESUS' NAME!

You will not falter nor shall you flounder. God is activating helpers now—your answer is about to arrive! Give Him glory and praise His holy name, for this starts NOW, says the Lord! Receive in the mighty name of Jesus Christ and get ready to TESTIFY! Glory to God! We thank You, Lord.

We both immediately received the word and started thanking the Lord for bringing it to fruition in our lives. Yes, Lord!

My daughter looked at me and said, "Soooo, should we just stay parked here until we get a call from someone?" At that moment, the oil-change message on our car flashed on again. I had been ignoring it, but I felt that right then, we needed fresh oil for our mission, physically and spiritually. We headed over to the local QuickLube. I asked the incredibly nice man to go ahead and check my tires, I had been hearing a weird sound, and he checked a few other miscellaneous things that had been bothering me. He did it graciously and even gave us a discount. Thank you, Jesus!

We got back into the car and twisted and turned through a small shopping center's parking lot. Then we found ourselves in front of a diner. My daughter said, "I'm craving eggs." This was so unlike her. She hates the things, but my stomach was growling as well. Before we exited the car, we called the retreat center and made our apologies for not being able to make it. They were extremely gracious, and we grabbed our face masks, locked the car, and bounded toward the diner, to fill our stomachs and wait on the Lord before we journeyed any further. As I was about to step up to the entryway, my phone rang. I glanced at the number. It was from Indiana, and it was an unknown number. I tried to ignore it, thinking that it was someone trying to sell me something, but as soon as I lifted my finger to ignore it, the Holy Spirit instantly played back part of the prophetic word that we had heard just thirty minutes earlier.

> I prophesy God is about to put your name on the heart of someone who can help you. He's going to drop your name in the spirit of someone who can ADVANCE you, FUND you, GUIDE you, even ACCELERATE and ADVISE you—IN JESUS'S NAME!"

My heart was pumping in my ears as I answered my phone and said, "Hello."

The lady's voice on the other end was kind and upbeat. "Is this Mary?"

I replied, "Yes, it is."

She then proceeded to tell me that she just "happened" to be flipping through papers from September and realized that she needed to follow up with me on getting my book published. Then she asked, "Are you ready to publish?"

This question rang in my ears. In that moment, I knew that even the twists and turns that had got me to the entrance of the diner on November 2, 2020, had been orchestrated by the Lord. The Holy Spirit had been guiding us all along because we surrendered to him. Wow! So many times along the way, I felt like Noah in the book, *The Notebook*, when he bluntly asked the girl he loved, "What do you want? What do you want?" He just wanted an answer from the girl, and I just wanted an answer from the Lord, but the Lord wanted me to learn to listen to his still, small voice.

The girl in the movie had responded to Noah by saying, "It's not that simple!" But as children of God who walk with the Holy Spirit leading us, it can be that simple.

And your ears shall hear a word behind you, saying, "This is the way, walk in it," when you turn to the right or when you turn to the left." (Isaiah 30:21 ESV)

- You may feel this way today. Crying out to the Lord saying, "Lord, what do you want me to do? How do I handle this situation?" He is there even when we don't see it and maneuvering things for your good. I encourage you to ask the Holy Spirit to help you quiet your mind right now and say out loud, "Jesus, I trust you!"
- Feel free to receive this prophetic word for yourself and to ask the Holy Spirit to lay your name on the heart of someone who can help you.

_____

_____

_____

_____

_____

Chapter 9

ARISE AND GO

---✦---

The highways were deserted, And the travelers walked along the byways. Village life ceased, it ceased in Israel, Until I, Deborah, arose, a mother in Israel.

(Judges 5:6–7 NKJV)

Woman, arise! I heard this phrase in my spirit when I read about Deborah in Judges. It sounds dramatic and bossy, but I truly believe that is how the Holy Spirit wanted me to take it that morning. I was on my knees praying about what was next in the journey that the Lord had begun at the coffee shop on the previous day. It was initiated long before that, but it had just started to come into focus a bit more at that point. Wow! Not only that but I was so motivated and encouraged. The Holy Spirit was leading my steps, and the Lord had let me become very aware of it. However, by the time we got to a hotel in Redding, California, and had used hotel points to pay, I was becoming very aware of the shortage of money in our bank accounts, and I didn't know where in the world we should head from there.

For hours that night, I searched for a location to go next. I had heard the Lord clearly say that I should work on the book, but I wondered where we should go and what the next step was. As I lay there in bed searching through Airbnb's website, I heard the Holy Spirit say, *Relax. I brought you here so let me step it out for you.* I heard him—that's the truth of it—but I continued to battle my thoughts, which said, *You better be smart, logical, and be prepared.* Then I heard one of my favorite verses play in my spirit.

Trust the Lord with all your heart, lean <u>NOT</u> in your own understanding, In <u>ALL</u> your ways acknowledge the Lord, and <u>HE</u> will direct your steps.

(Proverbs 3:5–6 NKJV)

OK, Lord, I surrender to your rest and plans. I do trust you. Goodnight.

I woke up the next morning refreshed. I fell to my knees and heard the Holy Spirit say, "It's time for the Deborahs to arise." Now, Deborah in the Bible is so very cool. She was a prophetess and a judge during the time of the judges in Israel. She would sit under the palm tree of Deborah between Ramah and Bethel, in the hill country of Ephraim, and the Israelites came to her for judgment. Her story is about so much more than being a judge. She prophesied and told Barak, the commander of Israel's armies, to attack Sisera, the enemy. God destroyed Sisera and his entire army by using a woman named Jael. She drove a tent peg through Sisera's temple after he had fallen asleep. I know! That's disgusting, but how awesome that the Lord works through women who are willing to be his vessels of glory and to bring his glory.

After I heard the Holy Spirit say, *``It's time for the Deborahs to arise, ''* I jumped up and yelled, "Piper, it's time for Deborahs to arise!"

She nodded, not quite awake and said, "That's great mom."

I glanced back at the Airbnb website that I had scourged the night before. My eyes fell on a place in a town called Lookout, California. I hit "reserve for three nights" because that was all that was available. Then I looked at a map of the location. It was near a lookout tower on Timber Mountain in California. A couple of years earlier, I had worked as a newspaper reporter and interviewed a sweet elderly woman who had gone with her husband to work and live in the fire lookout tower at Timber Mountain in the 1940s. They lived in the tower and watched for any sparks from the train or fire for any other reason. She had a daughter, who was with them, and just a toddler at the time. The precious lady had also shared that she had miscarried a baby while living out by themselves on the mountain. She had always wanted to visit the location again. At that moment, I knew that I had to go there as soon as we arrived in the area. All of the sudden, my daughter, who gets all the messages from Airbnb, yelled, "Mom, Deborah has accepted your request to stay at her place."

Deborah! Yes, that's what I said. Can you believe that? The Lord is so precious. It was just one more reassurance that we were on the right path.

> My sheep listen to my voice; I know them, and they
> follow me.
>
> (John 10:27 NIV)

Then the Holy Spirit softly whispered, *Your writing is how you will arise like Deborah. I am calling my daughters to arise in their different callings. I have anointed and placed them here for this time in history, so arise, my love.*

- ~ Ask the Holy Spirit to reveal what you have been anointed for during this time in history. As I write that phrase, I am reminded of Esther, but I think we will talk about that in another chapter. Blessings!

_____

_____

_____

_____

_____

Chapter 10

MAHANAIM BASE CAMP - LOOKOUT

And we know that God causes everything to work together for the good of those who love God and are called according to his purpose for them.

(Romans 8:28 NLT)

We drove the back roads from Redding, California, through the beautiful town of Burney Falls, and past old western-looking towns until we came to a little local market that looked like it had been there since the Oregon Trail days. There was a T in the road, and we took a left and headed out into a valley with mountains on either side. This gorgeous drive took my breath away. We saw Mount Shasta rising with its snow capped top in the distance. We weren't sure where this was leading, but we knew that the Lord had orchestrated it.

One mile at a time, the anticipation grew, and then we were at our destination: the little town of Lookout, California. It was adorable and tiny. The location of our Airbnb was the local historic grange from back in the days of community meetings, dances, and much more. Across from the historic building was a barnlike structure, which looked like the set of *Little House on the Prairie*. On the top of it, the sign read, "Blacksmith." If I remember correctly, there was a livery building right next to it. By now, you know that I was getting excited as I imagined the people who walked these streets a hundred years ago.

I glanced back at our lodging for the next three days—a building that rose two stories in front of me and had a basement entrance on the side. I noticed a car sitting there. A sweet looking woman was standing outside as well, and we exchanged smiles as Piper and I exited the car. She came up and welcomed us, and before we knew it, all three of us hugged in greeting. Piper and I being huggers, we thought this was wonderful. This loving lady, who I presumed was Deborah, told us that she would take us on a tour of the lodging and explain how everything worked. How precious she was. Greeted with homemade goodies and an amazing espresso machine, we thought we were in heaven. It was definitely a perfect place for me to write. Instantly, we knew that Deborah was a kindred spirit. We started to visit and talk about the Lord. She explained that the name of the building was Mahanaim Base Camp and that the word *Mahanaim* meant *angel encampment* in Hebrew. The word was used in Genesis when Jacob was met by the angels of God.

An angel encampment was exactly what I needed to get back to writing and resting in the Lord. Only he could have orchestrated this divine encounter. We visited with our new friend and listened to our favorite worship songs together. Then she prayed over us. Of course, this was not a normal arrival at an Airbnb, but it was so supernatural, and the Holy Spirit was all around us. What more could we want?

After two days of good writing and sleeping on a cloud in that peaceful place, Piper and I decided to go exploring to see if we could find the old lookout tower that the lady, whom I had interviewed years earlier, had told me about. Not exactly sure of the precise location we launched out on our adventure. We drove and drove and finally narrowed down the location. It was magnificent. The view from the lookout tower was a panoramic 360-degree view, which had Mount Shasta on one side and Mount Lassen on the other side. We took pictures and lazily enjoyed all that the lookout had to offer. After about forty-five minutes of exploring, we climbed back into the car and made our way back down the mountain. When we finally got close to town, our cellphone reception came back, and messages from my son, who was still at missions' school, came flooding in.

Curious about what it could be, I quickly called him back. He was very excited about his experience and all that the Lord was doing in his life. He said, "Mom, there are about five of us that don't have anywhere to go for Thanksgiving break. I told them you could find us a place. Is that all right?"

"Of course!" I exclaimed. There was no way I was going to say no to my son and his ministry friends. "I'm on it." He was so thankful, and we got off the phone. This began my prayer of, *Lord, where can I find a place for all of these people to go for a couple of nights? Please help again and provide a place. Thank you, Father.*

We were headed back to the grange for something to eat, but instead, we decided to drive a little further to the market that we had passed on our way. As we pulled in, we saw the sign to Deborah's house and decided that after we grabbed food, we would call and see if her invitation to visit was still open. We did, and she was overjoyed for us to stop by and have a latte. Oh, yeah, that's the way to my heart.

She warmly welcomed us, and we joined her at her table and talked non stop about all that the Lord had been doing. We shared about finding the lookout tower. Then I told her about my son's call, and we all prayed for the Lord to make a way. We were saying goodbye and heading out the door when a tall, kind man with a white beard appeared at the door. Deborah introduced us to him as her husband, Ron, whom we quickly called Papa Ron because of his all-inclusive, loving nature like a papa. We hugged them goodbye and headed back to the Airbnb.

Piper and I rested for the night and again slept soundly in peace for our last night at Mahanaim (the angel encampment). The next morning, we awoke to a text from Deborah. It said that she and Papa Ron had prayed about it and that they wanted to offer their home to all the kids from the missions' group and us for Thanksgiving. That was four nights and all the fixings.

We were in shock and so very thankful that God had done it again. We had just met this amazing couple, and they were God's gift. They were willing to be used by the Lord to meet a group of missionaries' needs. What precious people the Lord brought into our lives.

How good and pleasant it is when God's people come together. He meets all our needs according to his glorious riches in Christ Jesus. I just can't make up how good and wonderful our Father is.

- Ask the Holy Spirit to remind you of a time when you were in trouble or in need, and he came through for you.
- He never leaves us. When do you sense his presence the most?

~ Ask him what promise he wants to remind you of today and then write it down so that you can declare it and be reminded of it over and over.

_____

_____

_____

_____

_____

Chapter 11

ASSIGNMENTS

If you keep quiet at a time like this, deliverance and relief
for the Jews will arise from some other place, but you and
your relatives will die. Who knows if perhaps you were
made queen for just such a time as this?

(Esther 4:14 NLT)

Most of us have heard the story of Esther many times and have
just brushed it away as if it was only meant for someone who
has a huge call on her life—someone like Esther, who is
royalty or set apart for something special. Today, I want to put before you
the following question: What if? What if you have been selected to do
something significant in this hour of history? Let me go deeper.

While I was reading the story of Deborah in the last chapter, which I
highly encourage you to do, I noticed that when Deborah and Barak sang
their victory song, they pointed out that the tribe of Benjamin and the
commanders and the lawgivers out of Zebulun came to those who handled
the pen or stylus of the writer. However, the scripture goes on to ask the
tribe of Rueben the reason that they lingered among the flocks. Then to
the tribe of Dan, it asks why they stayed with their ships. The last part of
Judges 5:17 in the Amplified Bible says, "These came not forth to battle for
God's people." I wonder how many of us don't go forth to battle for God's
people. I mean, we see what Mordecai said in the first part of Esther 4:14,
where it says, "If you keep quiet at a time like this, deliverance and relief
for the Jews will arise from some other place" (NLT).

OK, I can almost hear some of you say, "Yeah, but she was saving an
entire nation of people. She was the queen." But let me point out that back
in the portion of scripture from Judges, each of the tribes mentioned had

jobs, callings, and purposes. The people of Benjamin were commanders, the people of Zebulun were writers, the people of Rueben were shepherds, and the people of Dan were sailors, fishermen, traders, and so on. We have all been anointed for purposes in our lives.

- What have you been anointed and gifted to do?
- What giftings, and talents?
- Are you using them for the glory of the Lord? Are you going forth to battle for God's people using your anointing?

_____

_____

_____

_____

_____

Chapter 12

ANGELIC GAS STATION

Don't forget to show hospitality to strangers, for some who
have done this have entertained angels without realizing it!
(Hebrews 13:2 NLT)

As I wrote this book, I went around and interviewed friends and
family who had stories that shared the supernatural theme of *you
can't make this stuff up!* One of my favorite stories was from my Great
Uncle Jesse. He told me about a season of his life when he lived in California
during the 1960s. He was nineteen, and his parents lived in Texas, which was
where he met his fiancé. On his journey from California to Texas to marry
and bring back his bride, the most unique and supernatural event occurred.

Jesse was excited to drive his new car across the country, and he drove
at maximum speed across the long stretch from Reno to Las Vegas. About
sixty miles before Las Vegas, he realized that his gas tank was running low.
He hadn't been able to resist the long flat stretch of road that laid out before
him. The sports car had drained the gas at the higher-than-normal speeds.
Concern started to rise as he realized that he was in Death Valley, as the
deserted area was called. He knew that finding anyone or anything would
be almost impossible. Tumbleweeds, dust, cactus, and hot air were what
existed in the space between Jesse's destination and where he currently sat.
Quickly, as he was used to doing, Jesse cried out, "Oh, Lord, please let me
not run out of gas, or let me find a gas station."

His father had given him his Flying A gas card to fill up his tank with gas
on the trip, but he wondered what the odds were of finding a Flying A. He
would just be happy finding any place at all that sold gas. At this point, even a
lone home would be a sight for sore eyes. Maybe he could see if they might have
a jerrican of gas on hand for a tractor or their vehicle. Hopefully, they would

share with a stranded stranger. About the time that he started this train of thought, there was a faint light far in the distance. *Is it a light? Yes*, he thought. *Oh, Lord, please let this be somewhere or someone with gasoline.* The light grew as he inched closer and closer. The place came into focus, and his heart raced at the sight. Not only was it a gas station in the desert but none other than a Flying A. Wow!! Jesse was so thankful. He thought, *Praise God! Lord, you are amazing.*

He pulled up, and a dark-haired man stepped up and said, "How can I help you?" The man had a little scruff on his chin and wore coveralls. Jesse immediately told the man that he needed a fill-up, to which the dark-headed stranger said, "Absolutely! It's cold out here this evening. Why don't you go in and warm yourself by the potbellied stove inside? I'll tend to the car."

It was very cold out in the desert night air, so Jesse took the man up on his offer. He nodded, shut the car door behind him, strode over to the building, and pulled open the squeaky door. Immediately the warmth of the black stove began to warm him as he caught sight of an older man sitting in a chair next to the stove. He wore worn overalls and held a cane in front of him between his knees; however, it was the almost floor-length white beard, which hung softly from the kind-faced man's chin, that stunned Jesse. The old man looked into Jesse's eyes and said, "It's a cold night out here in the desert, isn't it?"

Jesse replied, "Yes, sir," as the older man stood, the chair sighed as he rose. The man made his way to the counter and slid behind the old cash register. Jesse pulled out his Flying A credit card and paid for the gas. He nodded at the older man and said, "Thank you, and have a good evening." To which the older man said, "You too, son."

Jesse jumped back in his car and pressed the gas pedal so that he could be on his way to see and marry his sweetheart. He couldn't quit thinking about the goodness of God, who had provided the gas station with the unique man inside. God was so good. He had to tell his beautiful wife-to-be as soon as he saw her. He thought that they might be able to stop back by the little gas station on their way back to California.

And that is exactly what they decided to do. A few days later, the in-love couple hit the road and headed for their new life in California, as man and wife. They were so excited, and he couldn't wait to see the little gas station with the potbellied stove and the unique old man whose beard hung to the floor.

They spent that night in a town along the way. The next morning, before he thought about it, he had filled his gas tank on their way out of town. When he realized that he wasn't that far from the quaint station he had discovered on his journey before, Jesse determined that they would stop anyway. He felt that Linda, his wife, just had to see the place. She would think it was so neat. When they got closer and closer to where the little gas station had been, it wasn't to be found. They drove back and forth on the same road that Jesse had traveled while on his way to Texas, but there was no gas station. Surprised and a little disappointed that Linda wouldn't be able to see this miracle gas station in the middle of the desert, they started talking about the place and the men that had been there. They wondered if the whole experience could have been more than just a neat place with unique characters. Could it have been a supernatural encounter with the angelic? What a thought!

About a month later when the credit card bill came to his father, Jesse told his parents about the encounter. His parents were very familiar with supernatural happenings in their lives, as ministers of the Kingdom of God. Jesse's father called his son and said, "Son, I have looked through the transactions on my gas card bill, and there is no charge at all from your trip through Nevada."

- I just want to drop this thought for you to contemplate in your heart. Could you have entertained strangers in your life who could have been angels?
- Ask the Lord to make you more aware of all the ways he's working in your life?

I'll share a very cool story from Acts with you in the next chapter. It will give you a glimpse into the angelic world and the peace that comes when angelic assistance is active in your life.

Chapter 13

SLEEPING IN CHAINS

And when Herod was about to bring him out, that night Peter was sleeping, bound with two chains between two soldiers, and the guards before the door were keeping the prison.

(Acts 12:6 NKJV)

I have always found the story in Acts 12 absolutely fascinating. We just have to read the encounter to think through this amazing story.

Now about that time Herod the king stretched out his hand to harass some from the church. Then he killed James, the brother of John with the sword. And because he saw that it pleased the Jews, he proceeded further to seize Peter also. Now it was during the Days of Unleavened Bread. So when he had arrested him, he put him in prison, and delivered him to four squads of soldiers to keep him, intending to bring him before the people after Passover. Peter was therefore kept in prison, but constant prayer was offered to God for him by the church. And when Herod was about to bring him out, that night Peter was sleeping, bound with two chains between two soldiers; and the guards before the door were keeping the prison. Now behold, an angel of the Lord stood by him, and a light shone in the prison; and he struck Peter on the side and raised him up, saying, "Arise quickly!" And his chains fell off his hands. Then the angel said to him, "Gird yourself and tie on your sandals"; and so he did. And he said to him, "Put on your garment and follow me." So he went out and followed him, and did not know that what was done by the angel was real, but thought he was seeing a vision. When they were past the first and the second guard posts, they came to the iron gate that leads to the city, which opened to them of its own accord; and they went out and went down one street, and immediately the angel departed from him. And when Peter had come to himself, he said, "Now I know for certain that the Lord has sent His angel, and has delivered me from the hand of Herod and from all the expectation of the Jewish people."

So, when he had considered this, he came to the house of Mary, the mother of John whose surname was Mark, where many were gathered together praying. And as Peter knocked at the door of the gate, a girl named Rhoda came to answer. When she recognized Peter's voice, because of her gladness she did not open the gate, but ran in and announced that Peter stood before the gate. But they said to her, "You are beside yourself!" Yet she kept insisting that it was so. So they said, "It is his angel." Now Peter continued knocking; and when they opened the door and saw him, they were astonished.

(Acts 12:1–16 NKJV)

OK, can I just point out a few astonishing points here? First, the Jewish King Herod stretches out his hand to harass some of the church. Can we relate to anything like this? Fortunately, most of us haven't been threatened to be killed or even arrested, but we are experiencing more and more restrictions and resistance for being Jesus's followers, but can you imagine? He killed James, who was the brother of John. Both of these men were disciples who walked with Jesus. Then Herod sees that the religious Jewish people liked that he killed James so much that he seized Peter also. What? I know they disagreed and hated Christ's followers (aka Christians), but they were happy to kill them and seize more of them to be killed.

Wow! Friends, we have to know our Jesus to endure persecutions. I know this is strong, but seriously, we have to read the Word and know

Jesus deeply to be able to withstand experiences like those of the apostles. Jesus himself reassures us in John 16:33, "I have told you these things, so that in me you may have peace. In this world, you will have trouble. But take heart! I have overcome the world" (NIV).

Let's pop back into Acts 12. After King Herod arrested Peter, he decided that he should wait until after Passover to bring him before the people. He put him in the custody of four soldiers—y'all four soldiers! Peter was bound with two chains between two soldiers, and two were on guard in front of the door.

Can you imagine being in this situation? Peter was sleeping! Ummm … I'm not sure that I could relax, but Peter did. Wow! What confidence he had, knowing that if God wanted him there, he couldn't do anything about it but trust and rest. If God didn't want him there, only God could handle the situation and deliver him. Either way, Peter knew God was in control. He only needed to be confident in that and rest. No matter what happened, he would rest in God's sovereignty.

I just have to stop and be wrecked by the Holy Spirit because I want that kind of confidence in God's control of my life. I think Peter had learned this lesson with Jesus when the storm hit their ship, and all the disciples were terrified. But where was Jesus? He was asleep and resting in the back of the boat, but that's a story for another chapter.

- Right now, let's talk to Jesus and say, *Lord, we give you everything we are, have, love, and hold dear. We don't want to hold anything back. Plans of our own are fleeting, as only you know what tomorrow holds. It's not only tomorrow, but you know what the next second holds.*

_____

_____

_____

_____

_____

Chapter 14

SLEEPWALKING

Now behold, an angel of the Lord stood by him, and a
light shone in the prison; and he struck Peter on the side
and raised him up, saying, "Arise quickly!" And his chains
fell off his hands.

(Acts 12:7 NKJV)

As we pick up where Peter was snoozing, chained in handcuffs
to two guards, and guarded by two more guards in front of the
door, we find one little sentence in Acts 12:5 that gives a fuller
picture of what was happening to Peter and this agenda to have him killed.
These words also remind me of a picturesque explanation of what really
goes on in all of our lives.

For we wrestle **NOT** against flesh and blood, but against
principalities, against powers, against the rulers of the
darkness of this world, against spiritual wickedness in
high places.

(Ephesians 6:12 KJV).

So according to Ephesians 6:12, we are not fighting physical people,
authorities, organizations, etc., but we are actually fighting the enemy and
his demonic powers. There is *absolutely no way* for me or you to fight a
demon in our own strength, and I don't think this is on any of our agendas
or part of our desires. However, if we recognize that what we are fighting
against is Satan's agenda and that he has principalities, powers, and rulers
of the darkness of this world on active duty, we can address the situation
appropriately.

This is exactly what the church (aka Jesus's followers and Kingdom Ambassadors) was doing as soon as Peter was thrown into prison. They were praying. They recognized just as the napping Peter did, what that they could do to assist Peter was to invite God into the situation. They had to pray and ask God to send deliverance, use the situation, to do his will on Earth in Peter's situation as he saw fit, and further his Kingdom agenda. That is exactly what they did. As we stand together in faith, we must believe that God will do what he says he will do. As we pray, the Bible says that we put demons to flight. The more people that pray together, the more the multiplication factor hits turbo mode, and demonic powers begin to be flung out of the situation. Hallelujah!

As the church was praying, Peter was snoozing, and demons were attacking. Suddenly, the situation was primed and ready for the miraculous. Then bam! An angel of the Lord was standing next to Peter. Did he come out of nowhere? No, this angel came as a result of the spiritual atmosphere being primed and ready for God's will to be accomplished. Believers were in agreement, and Peter was resting in God Almighty's sovereignty, to do what was needed to accomplish his perfect will.

An angel stood next to Peter. Let me tell you that in my own opinion and deduction from the text, Peter must have been completely at rest because this magnificent angel had to jab Peter in the side to get him to wake up, not to mention that the verse says a light shone in the prison before the angel ever struck Peter's side. I'm sorry, but I have to just say LOL. I know that's text talk, but it perfectly describes the peace that was over Peter. Anyway, I must carry on with how this great story played out. Let's look at this section of scripture again.

> Now behold, an angel of the Lord stood by him, and a light shone in the prison; and he struck Peter on the side and raised him up, saying, "Arise quickly!" And his chains fell off his hands. Then the angel said to him, "Gird yourself and tie on your sandals"; and so he did. And he said to him, "Put on your garment and follow me." So he went out and followed him, and did not know that what was done by the angel was real, but thought he was seeing a vision. When they were past the first and the second

guard posts, they came to the iron gate that leads to the city, which opened to them of its own accord; and they went out and went down one street, and immediately the angel departed from him.

(Acts 12:7–10 NKJV)

So after the angel struck Peter on the side, and then basically picked Peter up and told him, "Get up fast. Here, I'll help you get started." Then Peter's chains fell off his hands, which had to have been loud. The angel then proceeded to tell Peter, "Get ready, Peter. Put on your sandals and robe. Now follow me." Of course, Peter obeyed the angel's requests. As Peter followed the angel out of the prison, I find this next section of scripture fascinating. Let's dissect it.

First, Peter didn't even understand what was going on and whether what the angel did was real. Peter was so familiar with visions from the Lord that he thought he was seeing a vision before thinking that it could have been real. I have to pose this thought to you: Do you ever have moments when the Lord protects you by leading you around in an out-of-body feeling or like you are just going through the motions as he works on your behalf? I think this might be how Peter felt. Like when you have surgery, if you were awake, you would be scared to death, and you might even fight the surgeon. When you are sedated, you wake up, and it's over. I don't know if that is the best illustration, but it came to mind. I'm sure you get the gist. OK, let's move on.

Second, with Peter following closely behind in a daze, the angel not only walked out of the prison cell but also passed the first set of guards and then the second set. He proceeded to an iron gate that led to the city, which opened by itself! Are you serious! Then they walked out and down one street, and then the angel disappeared. I know! Peter was in a daze, and now it appeared that he was led out into the middle of town and left there to figure it out. I think this is a great place to transition to the next chapter.

- Is there anything in your life that you feel chained to right now? It could be a circumstance, thought pattern, shame, fear, etc. Identify and write it down here.

~ Now say, *Father, forgive me for believing the lie that says I have to stay bound to this _____. Help me believe that you love me and have a plan to jailbreak me free from all bondage and lies of the enemy. I come out of agreement with _____ today.*

~ Next, ask the Lord what he wants you to believe in place of the lie. *Lord, what do you want to give me in place of _____?*

~ Now you get to receive your freedom by saying and declaring with confidence, "I receive _____" [whatever the Lord gave you in the previous step].

_____

_____

_____

_____

_____

Chapter 15

SUPERNATURAL MANEUVERING

---◆---

But they said to her, "You are beside yourself!" Yet she
kept insisting that it was so. So they said, "It is his angel."
(Acts 12:15 NKJV)

Peter was standing in the middle of the street in a foggy mindset,
and the angel had disappeared. Let's see what happened next.

And when Peter had come to himself, he said, "Now I
know for certain that the Lord has sent His angel, and
has delivered me from the hand of Herod and from
all the expectation of the Jewish people." So, when he
had considered this, he came to the house of Mary, the
mother of John whose surname was Mark, where many
were gathered together praying. And as Peter knocked at
the door of the gate, a girl named Rhoda came to answer.
When she recognized Peter's voice, because of her gladness
she did not open the gate, but ran in and announced that
Peter stood before the gate. But they said to her, "You are
beside yourself!" Yet she kept insisting that it was so. So
they said, "It is his angel." Now Peter continued knocking;
and when they opened the door and saw him, they were
astonished.

(Acts 12:11–16 NKJV)

After the angel disappeared, Peter finally comes to himself, and the entire experience now makes sense to him. He realized that the supernatural was involved and that God had not only delivered him from Herod but also reassured him that he no longer needed to worry about the expectations of the Jewish people. How many of us would benefit from that revelation? I know it's something I am becoming increasingly aware of after writing this book and going through the experiences that I am sharing with you—all of these *You Can't Make This Stuff Up* stories. I'm understanding more and more that when I rest in Jesus, he has my back. If I can release the outcome in confidence to God, his involvement, and his will being done, I can truly walk in freedom. My heart's cry is that I will continue to learn this more deeply and be able to "sleep" in any situation, as Peter did. As I read the scriptures, they describe events and encounters that reassure me that nothing is impossible for God.

This next part of the scripture makes me stand in awe of the supernatural the church in Acts experienced daily. Let me explain my train of thought. Peter came to the deep revelation that he had nothing to fear from Herod or the Jewish people. He then found himself at the house where the church was praying for him. A girl named Rhoda heard Peter's voice and got so excited that she ran inside and told everyone that Peter was outside, instead of letting him in. When she told everyone that Peter was outside, they all responded in a way that I find so very interesting. They said to her, "You are out of your mind!" But she kept insisting that it was so. They kept saying, "It is his angel!"

Now, what gets me intrigued is that they believed it was Peter's angel before they believed it was him in the flesh. Peter kept knocking on the door, and finally, they opened the door. When they saw Peter, they were astonished. I don't know, but I pose the point that just maybe the early church in Acts had enough experiences with the supernatural that seeing Peter's angel would have been more believable or more common than seeing Peter in the flesh and delivered from the hand of the enemy. So I remind us again, don't forget to show hospitality to strangers, for some who have done this have entertained angels without realizing it (See Hebrews 13:2 NLT).

~ Ask the Holy Spirit to show you ways that you can be more aware of His Kingdom Realm in your life today: *Open our spiritual eyes, Lord.*

_____

_____

_____

_____

_____

Chapter 16

VOICE OF BOLDNESS

And remember this: When people publicly accuse you
and forcefully drag you before the religious leaders
and authorities, do not be troubled. Don't worry about
defending yourself or how to answer their accusations.
Simply be confident and allow the Spirit of Wisdom access
to your heart, and in that very moment he will reveal what
you are to say to them.

(Luke 12:11–12 TPT)

I am going to share an experience that is ever so precious to me. My
beautiful niece is the main character in this chapter's story. Let me
describe this amazing, young woman, whom I adore. She is five feet,
four inches tall. She is a little spitfire with kindness and love for everyone
she meets. She is a ray of sunshine, and she has been such a blessing in
my life.

A couple of days ago, I received a phone call from my precious niece,
Emma. Her passionate voice was shaky as she immediately dove into
explaining an experience that she had just walked out of, which had caused
her to be all shook up. The encounter started at a major state university.
She walked to an area right outside of the university's chapel, where a
crowd had formed around a woman who was adamantly proclaiming that
everyone was going to hell. My niece continued to vigorously tell me about
this self-declared evangelist, who continued to spew hate.

My niece said, "Aunt Mary, my heart was racing, and my face was red.
I couldn't stand it, so I decided to just leave and not put myself under the
horrible words and unloving motive behind them, but as I turned to leave,
I felt an internal pull on my shoulder. It was like someone was nudging me

to go back and stand. So I did! I stood, and then words began to flow out of my mouth, and a silence fell on the crowd that had been yelling back at the lady in disgust."

My niece continued to tell me that she felt this righteous indignation rise within her. She said, "Aunt Mary, I couldn't stand that there were people who didn't know Jesus, and this is what they were hearing." She said that as the words came out of her mouth, she heard herself say, "That's not true. That's not my Jesus. Jesus loves us all and died for us all. We are all sinners gone astray. He died to take away the sins of the world." She went on to declare the love of Jesus, the Kingdom of God, that Jesus set the captives free, and that now there is no more condemnation for those who are in Christ Jesus.

When my niece was finished and worn out from retelling the event, I told her, "Sweetie, you just lived out what Jesus said would happen in situations like these, and I am so inspired by your willingness to stand up for who Jesus is."

She replied, "What? How did I live out what Jesus said would happen?"

Then I explained that in Luke 12:8–12, Jesus explained what happens when you stand boldly and declare that Jesus is God and love.

> I can assure you of this: If you don't hold back, but freely declare in public that I am the Son of Man, the Messiah, I will freely declare to all the angels of God that you are mine. But if you publicly pretend that you don't know me, I will deny you before the angels of God. If anyone speaks evil of me, the Son of Man, he can be forgiven. But if anyone scornfully speaks against the Holy Spirit, it will never be forgiven. And remember this: When people accuse you before everyone and forcefully drag you before the religious leaders and authorities, do not be troubled. Don't worry about defending yourself or be concerned about how to answer their accusations. Simply be confident and allow the Spirit of Wisdom access to your heart, and he will reveal in that very moment what you are to say to them.
>
> (Luke 12:8–12 TPT)

Now that we have read how this scripture played out in my niece's life, I want to pose another thought for us to ponder.

- Ask the Holy Spirit to remind you of the last time that you had the opportunity to stand up and freely declare in public that Jesus is the Son of Man, the Messiah. Maybe it was in school, at work, at dinner with friends, or during a political conversation. If you can't remember an opportunity, ask the Lord to make you more aware of opportunities—that they would flash like a bright light in your spirit. He will give you the words to say and the love to share with others.

I want us to be women and men who don't just read a Bible verse and then say, "Oh, isn't that great," but women and men who are proud to boldly declare that Jesus is Lord. I also pray that in doing this, we will also be people whom Jesus declares to all the angels of God that we are his. Amen!

_____

_____

_____

_____

_____

Chapter 17

GOD SPA

You shouldn't be amazed by my statement, "You all must be born from above!" For the Spirit-Wind blows as it chooses. You can hear its sound, but you don't know where it came from or where it's going. So it is the same with those who are Spirit-born!

(John 3:7–8 TPT)

My daughter and I found ourselves in Redding, California. We had dropped my son off at a mission school in Chico, California, visited with family, and worked on some research for writing. This research was a book of its own, with the events that were happening. I want to share just a couple of the *You Can't Make This Stuff Up!* moments that occurred along the way.

We were in Redding, California, for a three-night stint during the last week of November. We found a neat Airbnb. Little did we know how neat this oasis would be. The stop was in between saying goodbye to my son, as I wouldn't see him again until he got back from Mexico, in February and our return to Ron and Deborah's where we would stay for the next few weeks.. We two traveling writing girls were pulling up to a quaint Airbnb at around 8:00 p.m. We were not at all sure where our journey would lead us next. We weren't even sure where we would spend Christmas. At this point, the pandemic prevented us from seeing my parents, we were very far from Oklahoma, and we were in a rhythm of writing. We talked about this situation around and around. Have you ever been there before? Have you let options of what would be the best thing to do spin around until you just want to throw your hands up in the air? That is where we were. We finally stopped and prayed. "Lord, we don't know what to do or where to go at this point. Please lead us." I have to laugh because this is the way my daughter and I roll on a pretty continuous basis but I'm so glad we are getting quicker to recognize just pray.

As we started to unload the car, the Airbnb's hostess came out and introduced herself as Kim. She showed us the way around to the entrance. We introduced ourselves, chatted, and admired the beautiful landscape and woodwork that wrapped its way around the house to a small vineyard nestled in a spa-like atmosphere with mesmerizing garden lights. There was the faintest sound of water trickling at a rhythmic pace that played in the background. We turned and saw the cottage entrance to our home for the following two nights. In this short amount of time, we could tell that this sweet lady would be a dear friend and a kindred spirit indeed. We stood there, talked about the Lord and his goodness for quite a while, prayed together, and said our goodnight.

With such a welcome, Piper and I slept soundly and awoke refreshed. The lady had told us that she wouldn't be around until the day we checked out and to make ourselves at home, which we enjoyed doing. We rested, prayed, and sought the Lord for what our next step would be. We wondered where we would spend Christmas, which was quickly speeding up to us.

On the last day of our retreat, we awoke to a text from the kind lady, saying that she was back and that she would love to say goodbye before we hit the road. Pulling our suitcases around to the car, we popped open the trunk as a female voice came from the front of the building. "Hello, how are you? I wish we had more time to visit, but I have something strange to ask you. Would you two be available to house-sit for us at Christmas? We are going to spend it in Oregon with my family and have been worried about what to do with the house and the Airbnb. Is there any chance that you two would be interested in house-sitting? I will have the entire house decorated, and you can invite your family and just enjoy our home for the holidays."

Well you know my first thought was, *You can't make this stuff up*. Sure enough, you can't! Piper and I were almost in tears as we immediately responded with, "Yes," in unison. We explained to her that we had been praying about what we were going to do for Christmas, and here it was. Peace flooded our souls as we recognized once again, how precious and providing our Jesus is. He goes before us, and his spirit leads us to the places that we need to go.

So many times, I find myself wondering what in the world I will do next and why in the world I am in a certain place with certain people, and all along, he has been in control. I love him, and he knows me. I don't always feel like I deserve it. I even have times when I feel distant from his voice, but he always comes through, and I find myself again saying, *Lord, you are so good. You are always on time and always working things for my good and your glory.* I am now good friends with this precious Airbnb owner, and I pray for her regularly as I know she does for me. *Thank you, Lord, for another encounter and you-can't-make-this-stuff-up experience.*

I was praying for a scripture to start this story with, and the Holy Spirit led me to go to my devotional for the day. The first verse was the one I used.

> You shouldn't be amazed by my statement, "You all must be born from above!" For the Spirit-Wind blows as it chooses. You can hear its sound, but you don't know where it came from or where it's going. So it is the same with those who are Spirit-born!

After reading these words and thinking about the encounter in Redding, I realized that this is what a Spirit-born person's life looks like. We track differently. We don't make sense to the world. This new birth is mysterious, and the way we live is too. We live by the movement of the Holy Spirit. Even if we don't understand when and how it happens, we are willing to flow with and where he leads.

This scripture verse is found in the middle of the Jewish religious leader Nicodemus's conversation with Jesus. Nicodemus was trying to figure out Jesus, his miracles, his authority, and his power. He wondered if Jesus was God. He didn't know how he could be sure. Nicodmus was confused when Jesus spoke those words. Nicodemus replies, saying, "I don't understand what you are saying!" The commentary in the Passion Translation says, "If our new birth is so mysterious, how much more will be the ways of living each moment by the movement of the Holy Spirit? You can then understand why Nicodemus was confused, for he took Jesus's words at face value and couldn't see a deeper meaning."

Jesus had even started the conversation with Nicodemus with these words: "Nicodemus, listen to this eternal truth: Before a person can perceive God's kingdom realm, they must first experience a rebirth." This brings me to say, if you haven't been reborn, believed that Jesus Christ died on the cross and shed his blood for the forgiveness of your sins, know that Jesus is the only way, truth, and life, have a conversation with him right now. Be honest with Jesus and tell him you need him, you want him, and you want his Holy Spirit to lead the way you live. It won't look like my life or anyone else's. He created you with a special plan and a life custom-designed for your personality. I can guarantee you this: It is so custom tailored to you that it will be the only life that will satisfy you from now into eternity. Oh, how he loves you! He wants you to live a life of peace and joy. I bless you to be at peace and full of joy.

- If you haven't told Jesus you believe in him and want him to be the Lord of your life, take time right now to do so. If you need a refreshing and refocusing of your relationship with him, do that right now as well. Remember, he is there with open and waiting arms and is ready to start this amazing adventure journey with you.

_____

_____

_____

_____

_____

Chapter 18

SUNDIAL BRIDGE

Everyone enjoys giving great advice. But how delightful it
is to say the right thing at the right time!

(Proverbs 15:23 TPT)

My cousin, James, and I were in Redding, California, walking
around at the Sundial Bridge. We were admiring the
architecture and talking about all the people who were out
and about to see the Christmas lights' display at the park. We noticed two
young guys in their mid-to-late twenties, who had matching black T-shirts
with a unique design on the front of them. A gold crown stood out on
a black background and had the word "FOUNDED" printed under the
crown. It caught my eye. I continued to watch the two guys as they took
pictures for some sort of advertisement, which I assumed was to promote
the shirt. My curiosity was piqued, and I started questioning out loud
and asked my cousin if he thought they were possibly a ministry group.
Then I asked him what he thought the word "FOUNDED" meant. He
entertained all my questions, but it was to no avail, and eventually, we
wandered back across the large bridge and forgot about the young men
with the cool shirts.

I wondered what my deal was and why I was so fascinated with what
they were doing. There had been people everywhere, but I had zoned in and
become intrigued. We stopped in the middle of the bridge and watched
some guys who were finishing a day of fly-fishing. Then out of the corner
of my eye, I noticed two black shirts approaching us in the middle of the
crowd. I started whispering aggressively to my cousin, "Those guys are
coming by. Should we say something?" He turned around, saw the two
guys, but hesitated to say anything to them. I wanted him to say something

instead of me, but the guys had already passed by us, and we were going to miss our chance. My curiosity and excitement to find out what they were part of was making a crescendo.

I was about to call out to them when all of a sudden from next to me, there came a bold yell from my cousin. "I like your shirt, man!" It felt like we were watching in slow motion as both guys turned around and seemed taken aback when they realized that we were talking to them.. One responded with a half-nod and quirky smile.

That was a bit disappointing, but immediately, the other guy pivoted, reached up, put his hand on his buddy's shoulder, and said, "Go tell them about what you are doing." They then made their way over to us and told us their two powerful testimonies about being delivered from lives of addiction, imprisonment, and thoughts of suicide. They explained that Jesus spoke to their hearts with his all-consuming love and connected them to people, places, and experiences that led them into freedom. Jesus showed both of these young guys how much he loved them and that he would go to any length to reach them, even a brutal death on a Roman cross so that he might bridge the gap between them and him.

We were talking with these young men when suddenly, my cousin began tapping me on the shoulder and saying, "Your Victorian people. Mary, the Victorian people on the bridge with a river on both sides … Mary!" He was so excited, and I wasn't getting it, or as my daughter and I say, "I wasn't picking up what he was putting down." Then all of a sudden I remembered!

About six months earlier, I had been praying when I saw both of us standing on a bridge. A river ran below as people dressed in Victorian clothes walked by us. It all came full circle when I realized why he was so excited and trying to get my attention. There we stood side by side on a bridge with a river running on both sides. Victorian-dressed carolers made their way from one side of the bridge to the other side. We were standing in the vision that the Lord had given me six months earlier. It was playing out exactly as the Lord had shown me. I was speechless as my cousin explained what was happening to the two guys, who stood with confused looks on their faces. Then as quickly and unexpectedly as the vision had happened, one of the guys looked straight into my eyes and declared, "This is a divine moment!" All I could do was nod and think about how amazing

God was. He was personal and specific, yet I had almost missed it. Thank goodness, I had shared the vision, and my cousin was with me to point the supernatural moment out to me. I was so thankful, and scriptures began to flood my mind and spirit of how good God was.

He is so involved in our lives if we will just perceive it. How pleasant and wonderful it is to have others who are sensitive to what the Holy Spirit is doing in and around us as well. It's so delightful when a friend says the right thing at the right time.

- Think about the people in your life whom the Lord uses to speak words of encouragement or point out when the supernatural is all around you. Who are they? Are you aware of and giving glory to the Lord for these moments?
- Let's pray. *Father, help us be aware of what you are doing in and among us. Let us give others timely words of encouragement as we also appreciate those who speak the right things at the right times in our lives. Thank you, Father, for fellowship, friendship, and family.*

_____

_____

_____

_____

_____

Chapter 19

FOOD YOU KNOW NOT OF

Meanwhile, the disciples were urging Jesus, "Rabbi, eat something." But Jesus replied, "I have a kind of food you know nothing about." "Did someone bring him food while we were gone?" the disciples asked each other. Then Jesus explained: "My nourishment comes from doing the will of God, who sent me, and from finishing his work."

(John 4:31–34 NLT)

After the amazing encounter on the bridge, which was literally a vision come true, we were on a Holy Spirit energy high. My blood was pumping, and connections with more of the family of God were being made. We followed them out to the parking lot, where we purchased their first T-shirt to support their ministry. This young man had obeyed what the Lord had told him to do. After that, we spent time in the parking lot talking about what the Lord was doing all over the world. We had the opportunity to pray with these young men and speak life over them as well.

Cars maneuvered their way in and out of the parking lot, and we stood in a circle with hands on one another's shoulders as we agreed in prayer over what the Lord was orchestrating and walking these young men into for the next season of their assignment. It was beautiful. Then our new brothers spoke over us as well and prayed. Then we said our goodbyes and went our separate ways in the busy parking lot.

As my cousin and I walked away, we both felt the Holy Spirit's fire in our bones. It was the excitement of knowing that the presence of the living

God was among us and was active. We were exactly where we should be for such a time as this. We were about our Father's business. We weren't ready to leave that high yet. At the same time, we burst out with similar exclamations, "We can't leave yet!" Then we laughed and walked back to the park, where we had just walked out with our newfound brothers. Wow! The energy was electric. As families and friends were headed in to see the Christmas light show, with joy and anticipation filling their eyes and voices, it felt like we were floating right past them, with a satisfaction that this world couldn't give. We had been starving before we had encountered the young men. In fact, we had been headed to find food out of the park, but all thoughts of that were gone now and were replaced with peace, joy, hope, excitement, and anticipation for what the Lord would do next.

It was about two weeks later when I was watching *The Chosen* (a TV series that I believe everyone should watch because … oh, my goodness it's *amazing*) with some more of our spiritual family members. The Holy Spirit opened my eyes to the meaning of John 4:31–34. It was the scene with the woman at the well. Jesus had already told her that he had living water that she knew not of and that would satisfy her forever. He also told her everything that she had ever done and that he had come to Samaria, a place and a people that Jews believed unclean, just to meet her. Jesus was about his Father's business. When the disciples walked up and saw Jesus talking with a Samaritan woman, they were stunned. Yet none of them dared to ask him why he was there or what they were discussing. Then the woman dropped her water jar, ran off to her village, and told everyone she saw to come to see Jesus, a man who had told her everything she had ever done. What an amazing story it is. She was the first evangelist and a woman to boot.

However, that isn't even what got me this time when watching this story. After the Samaritan woman began evangelizing, people came streaming out of the village to see Jesus. The disciples insisted that Jesus eat some food. Isn't it funny how we *insist* that the Lord do things in certain ways in our lives or the lives of others? The disciples went as far as to say, "Teacher, you must eat something!" (John 4:31 TPT)

Then Jesus responds to them by saying, "Don't worry about me, I have eaten a meal you don't know about." Now, I've heard the response Jesus gave to the disciples about food all my life, and I have even reasoned out what makes sense in this scenario. However, this time, the Holy Spirit quickly whispered, *That energy you felt on the bridge the other day is what "having food you know not of" is talking about.*

I thought, *That's what you felt, Jesus. You were energized and were satisfied by the Samaritan woman's belief and excitement to go share what you had done. We lost our appetites after sharing and praying with our brothers on the bridge. We only thought of what you wanted us to do next. We just wanted to marinate in what you had let us experience. That is what you were feeling. You were being about the Father's business and loving your people. It satisfied you as it brought her wholeness and life.*

As I pondered this thought of us bringing the Lord satisfaction, I went to the *Merriam-Webster Dictionary* to get a better idea of what the word *satisfied* meant. This is what I found.

> To be pleased or content with what has been experienced or received.

Here is an example used in a sentence.

It attracted an audience with wild <u>satisfied</u> looks of feeling they were at just the right place that opening evening in Manhattan.

This sentence hit the nail on the head. This is exactly how I felt when we were bursting with excitement to get back in there and see if there was more. Who cared if we didn't eat? We were at the right place, at the right time, and Jesus was too. He was there with us, and we felt him, wanted more of him, and were satisfied by him. Then when I realized how satisfied he felt at that moment the Samaritan woman got it made my heart flood with joy, hope, and excitement all over again. I'm reminded of the old song we used to sing at church when I was a kid: "In My Heart There Rings a Melody." The first part of the chorus goes like this:

> In my heart, there rings a melody,
> There rings a melody with heaven's harmony;
> In my heart there rings a melody;
> There rings a melody of love.

I think the composer had to have experienced the satisfying feeling of being at the right place, at just the right time with Jesus as well.

- I want to challenge you to pinpoint the last time you experienced this satisfying energy from the Holy Spirit. If it's been too long, ask the Holy Spirit of the living God to align you with what he's doing and where he is moving in your life. He is faithful, and he will reveal himself to you.
- Make a list of where you see him moving in your life. If you are struggling to come up with a list, ask Jesus to come into your situation, show you where he is working in your life, and teach you how to be more aware of his daily movement.
- We can stand on his promises like David did. In the later part of Psalm 62:2–3, David says, "God is my champion defender; there's no risk of failure with God. So why would I let fear paralyze me" (TPT). Ask boldly and expectantly for the Lord's satisfaction.

Chapter 20

CHRISTMAS TREE LIGHTS

I am Yahweh, your mighty God! I grip your right hand and won't let you go! I whisper to you: "Don't be afraid; I am here to help you!"

(Isaiah 41:13 TPT)

I want to share one of my dearest friend's Facebook posts, which I read today. It immediately hit my spirit as a revelation of Father God's love for us. He is so crazy about us and wants us to enjoy walking through life with him. Sometimes we work at it so hard and wear ourselves out. In reality, he is just looking at us and thinking, *You couldn't make me love you more. You are my child, and I love you so unconditionally, fully, and completely that there is nothing you can do that will sway it one way or the other. You are mine.*

This is my friend Sherra's actual wording from her Facebook page:

So my wonderful precious daughter "SURPRISED" me yesterday when I came home.

We have been slowly putting up our Christmas tree. Yesterday she took it upon herself to go find the lights and put them on the tree before I got home from work.

She found the "outside lights" of white hanging icicles and white cords to put on the tree first. Well of course she ran out and had to put a "multi-color" one on top! Yes ... it was a HOT MESS, but you, as a mother, you compose your face and "DO NOT SAY A WORD!!!" Right!!!

I was just going to wait till she went to sleep and "tuck" those extra strands in so we could at least put the ornaments on the tree without them falling off.

And then this morning I was reflecting on it and smiling at the innocence of her heart and the kindness she has to want to do something special for us. Love her so much. And then I think goodness … we all try to make this "perfectly decorated" looking tree and sometimes we try to look so "perfect" and put it together on the outside when it is really just a "mess" that we try and hide from others. God takes that mess and imperfections that we keep "tucking" away from others to see and He just sees beauty … thankful He sees the beauty in me even when I don't.

God bless each of you who read this.

I want to pose a question for you to think about: Have you been trying to make a perfectly decorated looking life? Have you been wearing yourself out being a "good Christian" or earning what you think are bonus points with God? All along, he just wants you to throw those hanging outside lights on the tree and enjoy your life. He thinks you are wonderful.

So go have fun with Jesus and enjoy your life, no matter how it may look. The joy of the Lord is your strength. God loves you and uses the surrendered life.

- Right now, list everything that you feel you've been disqualifying yourself with—all your imperfections, fears, plans, etc.—and hold out your hands in front of you. Pretend your hands hold all the things that you feel make you not good enough for God. Now, lift your hands and say, *Lord, here are all my flaws, fears, and imperfections* [whatever it is for you]. *I give them all to you, and I don't want to take them back.*

- Now ask the Lord, *Father, what do you want to give me in place of all this stuff, these lies?*
- Next, wait quietly and let him tell you. He will lay something on your heart that you can declare and pray about. For example, I recently gave him feeling anxious, and in return, I asked what he wanted me to receive. Immediately, I felt in my spirit the phrase, *restoring the Joy of your salvation.* It wasn't an audible voice but a still, small knowing in my spirit. Yes, I took that in place of that stinkin anxiousness.
- Once he gives you a word or phrase in place of the issues, I want to remind you again and again to "Declare it!! Declare it!! Declare it!!" Write it down and put it on your mirror, in your car, or as a phone reminder. You want this to become what you believe and know deep down. It will become who you are in Christ and what he says about you.

Blessings, my friend!

_____

_____

_____

_____

Chapter 21

PRAYER ANSWERED

It shall also come to pass that before they call, I will answer; and while they are still speaking, I will hear.

(Isaiah 65:24 AMP)

In the fall of 2021, I was in counseling school at the University of the Nations at YWAM Kona. It was week ten of school, and everything was moving smoothly along. I was attending classes that made us dig deep into our lives. We learned how to take one another as well as others through the healing process. It had been a busy morning, and finally, lunchtime had arrived. We all ran up to the cafeteria. I had my cell phone tucked into my back pocket. Then a most unfortunate event occurred, which I'm sure has happened to you or someone you know. I dropped my phone in the toilet. Goodness! I never knew how bad it was to lose a phone until I was without one in the middle of the Pacific Ocean and four thousand miles away from my family. It was miserable.

I decided that I needed to pray a specific prayer for a specific phone. I needed not only a phone but an iPhone because I needed to be able to use my iCloud account. I started asking the Lord to give me one, and exactly one week after I dropped my phone, I was sitting at a cafe table outside the coffee shop on campus. We were gathered around the table, all working on schoolwork, when a new friend of mine, who was from Germany, heard me say that I was praying for an iPhone. She energetically spoke up and said, "I brought an iPhone 7 with me to school. I have one. My brothers bought me a new one before I left Germany for school. I decided to bring my iPhone 7 and give it to whoever said they needed it first. Do you want it?"

My jaw dropped, and my heart swelled with thankfulness at how amazing and faithful the Lord is. He had set things in motion to meet my needs months before I had even arrived in Hawaii. It was just like Isaiah 65:24 said: "It shall also come to pass that before they call, I will answer; and while they are still speaking, I will hear" (KJV). I thanked this sweet friend for her giving heart and praised the Lord. I thought, *God, you did it again. Wow! I'm going to be praying specific prayers from now on. Thank you, Father. You are so amazing.*

- Have you seen the Lord provide an answer to your prayer request before you even knew to ask it?
- Let's stop and thank him again for all the needs—known and unknown—he has answered. He inhabits our praises and our thankfulness for all he has done in our lives.

_____

_____

_____

_____

_____

Chapter 22

FOLLOWING
THE PEACE

❖

I have told you these things, so that in Me you may have
[perfect] peace. In the world, you have tribulation and
distress and suffering, but be courageous [be confident, be
undaunted, be filled with joy]; I have overcome the world.
[My conquest is accomplished, My victory abiding.]

(John 16:33 AMP)

When you don't know what to do, what do you do? How do
you come up with the next step to take? Do you flip a coin,
or do you weigh the pros and cons? How confident are you
in that final result? Do you still play the scenarios over in your head? *What
if? Should I have?* How long does this go on until you finally cry out to
God and say, *Help me*? Like the scripture says, can we live in peace in the
middle of the world's tribulations?

Maybe you are quicker to switch than I am, but I'm sure as a human, you
too have found yourself in a place of panic, worry, or just plain needing to
make a decision and not having the foggiest idea of what to do. I'm also sure
that whether you are a longtime believer in Jesus or not, you have prayed for an
answer, a sign, or something to help you know what to do or where to go next.

Well, I was in one of those situations that was extremely important. I
knew that I could not do it without Jesus. I cried out for an answer, and
he gave me a couple of supernatural encounters and signs that confirmed
what I was to do in that particular situation. However, I soon found out
that the Lord was teaching me to be still and know him. He wanted me to
actively hear his still, small voice and not just the big signs and encounters.

One day, Jesus told people who were gathered at the Temple and asking if he was the Messiah or not, "My sheep listen to my voice; I know them, and they follow me" (John 10:25 NIV). How simple. He speaks, and we listen. He knows us, and we follow him. Scripture teaches us that his plans for us are good and will give us a hope and future. He is working all things for our good, his daughters and sons who love him and listen to his voice. So that part is reassuring, but sometimes, the Lord asks us to do hard things, which might even hurt our hearts.

This was where I started my journey of learning about what following the peace really meant. It took on a meaning that morphed into an adventure of supernatural proportions. After thirty-nine years of living a Christian life, I was plunged into a boot camp of what peace really was. My mindset said it should feel good, and things should all come together like a fairytale, but I was in for a shock. I want to clarify that it was the best thing that ever happened to me. Yes, it was a correction of sorts, but thank goodness for that. In Hebrews 12:5–6, the author reminds us, "And have you forgotten the encouraging words God spoke to you as his children? He said, 'My child, don't make light of the LORD's discipline, and don't give up when he corrects you. For the LORD disciplines those he loves'" (NLT).

Oh, how he loves us, sweet friend. I am reminded of the line in the song "Way Maker," which says, "Even when I don't see it you're working, even when I don't feel it, you're working. You never stop, you never stop working." Jesus is continually working on our behalf. This is what I discovered. We can ask all day long about what to do—*Lord, please give me a sign*—and sometimes, he *will* jerk us out of a situation so that we can heal and be rebooted. However, there is a knowing in our spirits that brings peace, which comes only from the Holy Spirit. It is not a happy feeling because sometimes the way the Shepherd is leading might require something hard from us. It might require giving something or someone up. Peace is what comes when we are in the presence of Almighty God. When we have handed him our issues or dilemmas, and don't take them back.

Let me explain in a different way. Just like when the disciples and Jesus were traveling in a boat, and a storm came up out of nowhere. The disciples thought, *Hey, we are all panicking out here. Where is Jesus?* He was asleep, yes, asleep on that same boat. He was resting while they were working themselves into an anxious knot. He had peace even in the storm because he also knew who was in control, so he rested, trusted, and had peace.

I have heard two analogies of how to walk in peace, and they are both very neat. I think about them when I start to take control of things myself. I'm not sure where I heard the first one, but it is like putting glasses on and looking through them. You can either put on the glasses of life, the world, your situation, your trauma, etc., and look at God through those glasses, or you can put on the glasses of God and look at life, the world, your situation, your trauma, etc., through him. I know this is a simple illustration, but sometimes, that's exactly what we need. A simple go-to that helps us stop and say, "Wait a minute. How am I viewing this situation, this decision? Am I dealing with it and then asking God to help, or am I handing this situation over to God and seeing it through his sovereign viewpoint?"

The other example of walking in peace was given to me by a friend's mother. We were sitting on a couch in her log cabin in British Columbia, Canada. She and I had stayed up talking about Jesus for hours. I'm pretty sure that it was around 2:00 a.m. when she summed up all we had shared about life and its quandaries. She looked at me pointedly and said, "Mary, I have found that when I'm working and trying to figure out how a situation will work or what I can do to fix something, God is resting in the wings and waiting for me to invite him in. But when I finally rest and hand it all over to him, he goes to work. I know this sounds too simple, but you have to decide if you believe his Word and who he is. You can't give anything to someone you don't truly believe can handle it." It wasn't long after this discussion that I read about the disciples on the boat during a storm. When they finally woke Jesus and said, "Help us," he got up, and there was peace. Let's rest with Jesus and learn to follow his peace.

_____

_____

_____

_____

_____

Chapter 23

TREASURE HUNT

Therefore thus says the Lord God, "Behold, I am laying in Zion a stone, a tested stone, A costly cornerstone for the foundation, firmly placed. He who believes in it will not be disturbed."

(Isaiah 28:16 NASB)

W ell, let me tell you a secret. I love researching ancestry, so when the opportunity to go to a Bible conference in Rochester, New York, popped up, I was all over it. Can you guess why? I wanted to take a much-awaited genealogy journey through locations that I had found in old family documents and pictures. Because I was raised in Arkansas, and most of my ancestral research was located around that area, I was so excited to get my feet on the ground in New York. Plus, I could make this a multipurpose adventure. My daughter and I would fly to Rochester and attend an amazing conference for three days, then my mom would join us, and we would drive down through the heart of New York together. The three of us would scout out our family line.

We started the journey, and on the second day of traveling, I realized that we were very close to something that I had found while flipping through one of our old black-and-white family albums. It was a brick and stone mill house that one of my family members had meticulously labeled in white ink on the thin, old, black album pages, "Briggs Mill—John Thurston built it." How exciting it was. We were just two miles from the exact location of where the old mill had been built. Hopefully, some remains were left.

I navigated the car around a large curve in the road. We were surrounded by large trees, which were close enough to reach out and touch.

We finally came upon the spot. There stood a historic general store/post office that was still in use. We had passed a cemetery with "BRIGG'S" written on the sign, so I knew we were close. We looked around for any resemblance of the mill from the old album. Across the street from the store, stood a lone backhoe in a coned-off area. It looked as if the old brick building behind the equipment was being renovated, but it wasn't an exact match, and I wasn't sure it was the correct building. My heart sank. I have to admit that I was very discouraged that the first location we had tracked down was a bust—ugh!

All three of us got back in the rental car. I tried to brush off the discouragement and quickly prayed, *Lord, please let us find the next spot.* As we traveled down the beautiful rural road during New York's golden fall, we noticed a historic, red schoolhouse, which looked like a scene right out of a Hallmark movie, nestled snugly at the base of a green hillside. I think a united sigh escaped out of our trio's mouths at the same time as we passed the school.

Immediately, my mother exclaimed, "Go back! I think they are having a historical society meeting at that school."

I responded, "Mom, there's no way they are meeting at 2:00 p.m. on a Sunday." Well, needless to say, Mom was right. We turned around and found a parking lot full of cars and a sign that read, "Historical Society Gathering Today! Come on in."

The school's doors were open, and we could hear fiddle music playing in the air. We were met by a sweet lady standing behind a table of apple cider jugs and apple cider donuts. Oh yeah! We had to be in an idyllic fall movie. The lady warmly asked us how she could help us and if we wanted any refreshments. I told her what we were doing, and she pointed at a gentleman who sat on a bench enjoying the folk group that was playing in the front of the old schoolroom. She told me that he was the historical society's president and that he had lived in the area for years. He would be able to point us in the right direction.

The gentleman had a cane next to him that he leaned into as he turned to see us approaching. His smile was big and welcoming. He warmly asked, "How can I help you, ladies?" I explained that we were doing ancestry on our family names—Waterman, Vanderzee, Shear, and Thurston. He pointed to the display cabinets that surrounded the room. He said that we would find it full of journals and papers of past teachers and prominent people of the area named Shear. My heart started to race as my eyes scoured over the documents. He was correct, and I felt that the hunt was on. I thought of all the years the old black album had been passed down from parent to child, with grandparents saying that someday someone would go find all these family locations. Here I was! Again, I whispered, *Thank you, Lord!*

I told our new friend about the mill that I had been disappointed not to find. He smiled and motioned for us to follow him to the front wall. In a wooden frame, there was a sketch of the same mill that was in our family album. He asked, "Is this the mill you are talking about?" Oh, my goodness, I can't tell you how happy I was. If I couldn't see the building in person, at least I was getting the chance to see that it was real and something important enough in the community to be sketched, framed, and hung in the local schoolhouse.

Then the kind gentleman said, "You know, I haven't been over there in years, but it should still be there. I know they were talking about renovating it a while back, but I would think it should still be standing." I immediately knew that I had been too quick to decide that the brick building we had seen wasn't Brigg's Mill. It was only under construction, and I hadn't dug deep enough. He continued by saying, "I tell you what, go back to where you were and look for a cornerstone. I remember there used to be one, but I can't remember the name on it. I will be done here in about an hour, and if you come back this way, I have a surprise for you." My heart was soaring, and we girls were so excited that we almost bolted out of the beautiful little schoolhouse.

Back down the road, we had just gone down and around the big curve again. This time, we pulled up on the side of the brick building that had construction equipment around it. No one was working on a Sunday, but on the next day, it was sure to pick up. I was very aware of the divine timing on that as well. All three of us explored the building, searching for the cornerstone. We couldn't find it. We finally pushed on the old door that led to the middle of the mill house. The old beams stretched across the ceiling, and the woodwork and stonework were intricate. I was instantly transported to the time when my great-great-great-grandfather had been standing and looking up at his handiwork. How proud he must have been at this accomplishment. I was so proud of him almost two hundred years later.

I finally pulled myself back from the time gone by and started heading for the car where the girls were waiting. Then I glanced toward the front of the building. As I leaned against the electric pole, I saw that hidden by a concrete barrier, there was a large slab of dark charcoal stone. When I walked up to it, I realized that it had an inscription etched into it. It read, "Erected in 1844. By Wm. S. Briggs Esq. Capt. John Thurston. Builder." There it was; the cornerstone to this piece of history and my family. *Lord, you amaze me. Even these things you reveal to your children. You care about the things that I think are neat. Thank you, Lord, thank you.*

This discovery alone was the treasure chest that I had been searching for, but when we returned to meet our new friend, he was waiting in the parking lot of the schoolhouse. He pointed to the gorgeous yellow house across the street and said that it was his home. Then he proceeded to tell us that he and his wife had restored and registered it on the historical registry. The kind gentleman gave us a look of satisfaction and exclaimed, "It's called the Israel Shear House. Your ancestor built it, and we restored it as close as we could to the original design and colors. Would you like to take a tour?" I'm pretty sure that my mouth was wide open in awe. Sure enough, we got to walk through every nook and cranny of Israel Shear's home. Later he told us where the Vanderzee family home was, which fulfilled every picture from the little family album. How amazing this journey was, with all the divine appointments and discoveries along the way. You just can't make this stuff up!

I felt like the Holy Spirit highlighted the cornerstone aspect of this story. *Encyclopedia Britannica* describes and explains a cornerstone this way: "Buildings were laid out with astronomical precision in relation to points of the compass, with emphasis on corners. Cornerstones symbolized 'seeds' from which buildings would germinate and rise." The cornerstone in my story was taken off during the reconstruction of the building, and was haphazardly laid aside. The verse that I used at the beginning of this story is describing a tested and costly cornerstone for the foundation, which was firmly placed. This cornerstone is Jesus! He is our cornerstone. He is a secure and true foundation for us to build our lives on. I love the last line of that verse, which says, "He who believes in it will not be disturbed."

(Isaiah 28:16 NASB) What a way to live: believing in Jesus and trusting that we won't be disturbed, because of him and what he did on the cross.

- Have you been living as if the cornerstone of your life is like the one I found taken off and haphazardly laying aside? Or are you living with the knowledge that the cornerstone you are building your life on is firm and secure, and it will not let you be disturbed?
- Ask the Holy Spirit to show you any areas where you need to lay down your false way of thinking and pick up your confidence in Jesus, the Lover of your soul. He is the one who wants us to see all the moments that make us say, "You can't make this stuff up. Only God can do this."

_____

_____

_____

_____

_____

Chapter 24

HAWAIIAN
CHURCH BELL

Know therefore that the Lord your God is God, the faithful God who keeps covenant and steadfast love with those who love him and keep his commandments, to a thousand generations.

(Deuteronomy 7:9 ESV)

We had just moved into our dorm room at the University in Kona, Hawaii. We were ready to tackle the school of counseling and all the unknowns of living in a community of missionaries for the next six months. Sunday approached, and we were dressed and ready for church. The question was, which one of the amazing local congregations would we attend? One of our roommates, a sweet lad, born in China and now attending school in the United States, told us that she rang the bell in the old bell tower every Sunday morning at the oldest church in Hawaii. It's called Mokuaikaua Church, and it was built in 1837; however, the congregation started meeting in 1820. So being the history and ancestry buff that I am, this totally intrigued me. Off we went to watch our friend ring the bell and get to know a little about the history of this amazing island, which we would be living on for the following six months.

When we arrived at the stone structure, we saw the congregation of people gathered under a pavilion, which had been built adjacent to the historic church. However, our friend walked into the old building, so we followed, as the large door squeaked. We three ladies walked up the rickety old stairs and made our way to the top, where we followed the original balcony, which was suspended around the sanctuary. The old church was made and decorated with koa wood, lava rock, and stone. A sense of awe and reverence filled me. I could just imagine bamboo rugs covering the floor as native Hawaiians sat listening to the message of Jesus almost two hundred years before.

We arrived at the final ascent to the bell, which was sitting silently at the top of the large steeple. My sweet friend in her floral dress grasped the rope that hung loosely. She was ready to pull it and ring the announcement that called everyone within earshot to gather and worship our Lord. Each pull almost lifted her slight frame off the ground. After the last ring, we made our way back down the aged walkway to join the others for service.

During the close of the service, a beautiful lady came up to the front and explained that she was a local historian and that after service, she gave tours of the old church building, a narration of the land's history, and information about the island's first missionaries and the building structure itself. So obviously, my daughter and I were staying for that. We gathered around the front door and then followed her into the sanctuary, where we sat in the pews made from local island wood.

As we sat and listened, she told of the missionaries who had landed and brought the black box with the real God in it, which of course was a black wooden box filled with black Bibles, the Word of God. She told the backstory of how the missionaries and their wives had set sail and spread the good news of Jesus to the native Hawaiians. Then she mentioned the name of the first missionary, Asa Thurston, whose wife was Lucy Thurston. My daughter's head whipped to look back at me, and I looked at her. *Did we hear that correctly? Are we here in Hawaii, a place we know nothing about the history of, learning that the surname of the first missionaries was the same as our ancestors from New York? What?* I asked all about these people who loved Jesus and the Hawaiian people so much that they left everything and everyone they loved to tell a group of people in a foreign land about how much Jesus loved them and that he died for them.

We returned to our room later that day, and I dove into finding the direct tie, if any, that we had to Asa and Lucy. I found that he was a very distant uncle but family indeed. So here we were, my daughter and I, in Hawaii, training for counseling so that we could take the freeing knowledge of Jesus and his love to the world as missionaries ourselves. I looked over my family tree and the ins and outs of how our sweet Lord had weaved a beautiful tapestry through the generations, wooing and loving each person, and the tears began to fall. There were times of hardship. Some were like the prodigal son and ran from the Lord for seasons of their lives, but the goodness and faithfulness of our God chased them down. He is going to do what he says in his Word. God is good and loves us, and as the song says, "He is jealous for me."

- Think back and ask the Holy Spirit to show you how he has blessed your generations. If you are the first believing person in your family, ask what your generational blessings are for you and future generations and list them below.
- How does that make you feel?
- Tell the Lord how thankful you are for your generational blessings. They may have trickled down for hundreds of years, or you might be the first one who is breaking off the old and walking in the new—all that God has in store for your children and their children, and to a thousand generations, just like God promises in Deuteronomy 7:9.

_____

_____

_____

_____

_____

Chapter 25

TELLING OUR STORIES

All at once, the woman dropped her water jar and ran off to her village and told everyone, "Come and meet a man at the well who told me everything I've ever done! He could be the Anointed One we've been waiting for." Hearing this, the people came streaming out of the village to go see Jesus.

(John 4:28–30 TPT)

I was fourteen when I did the monologue drama to this amazing story. If you don't know it, a monologue is a drama done all by yourself. In this particular drama, I played the part of the Samaritan woman and spoke in such a way that the audience "picked up" on what Jesus was saying to me by my words and actions. As a result, I've given this story quite a bit of thought and prayer.

It is such a beautiful story. As Jesus was launching his ministry, he made a point of going through Samaria, a place that Jews would not normally enter, just to have an encounter with this woman. This woman had been married multiple times, and she was desperate for some peace and hope, which she thought would be a long time in coming. However, one moment with Jesus changed her forever and made her the first evangelist. Yes, this woman ran back to her town after Jesus revealed who he was, and she told everyone, "Come and meet a man who told me everything I've ever done! He could be the Anointed One we've been waiting for." Because this Samaritan woman shared Jesus and the things that he had done for her, the people came streaming out to meet Jesus.

Wow! What a woman she was. As a fourteen-year-young girl, doing this drama meant a lot to me because I dearly loved my Jesus. Every time I acted this story out, I felt his love more and more. However, now as an adult, it really blows me away. I have had so many more life experiences where Jesus has come through for me. I have absolutely been amazed at how precise and detailed his love has been for me. Even when I don't deserve, feel, see, or even seek his help, Jesus is still there. He sits beside me at the well, saying, *I know what's really going on, and I can fix it if you will let me. I can refresh you today with living water, Mary. I love you! I am for you! I know you are confused and waiting for answers, but I am your answer—at this very moment, not tomorrow, right now. Receive a deep refreshing drink of living water right now, my love.*

As I typed that, I felt his Holy Spirit well up within me and say that this is why we share what he has done and is doing in our lives. We have to tell our stories, friends. We have to share how awesome our Jesus is and how much he loves us. He will hunt us down and come after us, just like he did the Samaritan woman. He went out of his way, into a taboo area, sending his disciples off to find food, just so that he could be alone with her. He wants alone time with me and you as well, so that he can tell us that he knows about what we are going through and that he has already done something about it. He wants us to get excited and go tell everyone we know. Come meet this man who changed my life, restored my joy, and gave me hope!

- In this world, we have troubles, stresses, and relationships gone wrong. Pretty much anything can hit our lives, just like the woman at the well experienced. But just like her situation, Jesus is here for us and wants us to drink from his living water, which always satisfies.
- When do you sense him with you? How do you drink of his living water?
- Read 1 Peter 5:7, which says, "Pour out all your worries and stress upon him and leave them there, for he always tenderly cares for you" (TPT).

- ~ Now close your eyes and imagine doing exactly what that verse says. What does it look like? What is Jesus doing with all your cares?
- ~ How can you tell the story of what Jesus has done in your life today?

_____

_____

_____

_____

_____

Chapter 26

IN THE ARMS
OF JESUS

But now, O Jacob, listen to the Lord who created you. O Israel, the one who formed you says, "Do not be afraid, for I have ransomed you. I have called you by name; you are mine."

(Isaiah 43:1 NLT)

A few months ago, I had the chance to work with some of the most amazing young women at a children's home. I spent four months getting to know these unique, funny, and loving girls. One of them was turning seventeen years old. On the morning of her birthday and visit from family, which is a big deal because they only get family visits once or twice a year, she woke early and asked if she could make pancakes for everyone's breakfast. I told her that she could. Then the Holy Spirit reminded me that she was having a family visit that day and that was probably why she couldn't sleep. So I began praying for this sweetheart and all the emotions that she must be feeling. All of a sudden, I felt the Lord nudge me to read her the day's devotion from the *Jesus is Calling* devotional book.

I headed down the hallway toward the kitchen with the devotional book in hand. As I walked, I felt the Lord drop the thought in my mind. *Did you ask me if I had anything to say to her this morning?* Immediately, my mind went to all I needed to get done before the rest of the girls in the dorm woke up, and I started making excuses as to why I didn't have time to go back to the office, unlock the door, and get all spiritual to hear a big word from the Lord. Then all of the sudden I found myself scooting to the bench in the dark hallway and plopping down right there. I closed my eyes and whispered, "Father, what do you want me to tell this precious young lady today?" I instantly saw a pacifier, and before I could wonder, an image unfolded. I saw a baby with that pacifier in her mouth being held tenderly, safely, and securely in a man's arms. It was clear to me that this man was Jesus, and he was holding this young lady. Then I heard the Lord whisper, *Tell her that I am holding her safe and secure. I am her father. I hold her, her identity, her future, and all she is worried about. If she will be still in my arms, I will pacify her every anxious thought. I will comfort her. Tell her to rest and go enjoy her day, knowing that she is held in my arms through it all.*

My heart raced, and I was so excited to pass these precious words along to her. As I entered the kitchen, she was already at work, preparing the special breakfast for her friends. While she was working, I shared the Holy Spirit's words. I could tell that she was happy to get the words but not sure that it was really from the Lord. I pushed on and read the daily devotional, which I was still clutching. I hadn't had a chance to read it myself, and we were both in for a treat. The words seemed to float off the page as I read, "Rest in the stillness of my presence while I prepare you for this day. Be still and know that I am God. There is both a passive and active side to trusting me. As you rest in my presence, focusing on me, I quietly build bonds of trust between us." (Jesus is Calling Devotional by Sarah Young)

This was a complete written and oral picture of what the Lord had just shown me, and I had told her. We looked at each other. We were in awe of how perfect the Lord was. She went on her visit and had a wonderful day resting in her Lord's arms. This was a wonderful twist but not the end. Our Jesus is so sweet. He not only reassured this sweet girl but also went the extra mile and reassured me that I had heard his voice. The next day was Sunday. We were dressed up, and I was strategically sitting where I had a good eye on all these amazing girls whom I was responsible for. The older girl from the day before was sitting up front and in the middle of a group of three girls.

The worship music faded out, and the pastor took the pulpit and as he usually did. An image that reflected his sermon popped up on the large screen at the front of the sanctuary. Low and behold, it was a black-and-white image of a sweet baby resting and sleeping soundly in the protective and secure arms of her father. The sermon title was "Resting in the arms of Jesus." Then as if an electric bolt had hit her, this young lady turned around and loudly exclaimed, "Ms. Mary, oh, my goodness!" All I could do was put my hand over my mouth to muffle my own squeak as tears slowly flowed down my cheeks. Oh, how wonderful you are, Jesus! You always come after the one.

- The Lord will never leave you nor forsake you. Take this time to thank him for always being there for you. Thank him for everything and everyone you can think of. Then give him your stillness, quietness, and space so that you can hear what he wants to tell you—how much he loves and calls you his.
- Write down all he tells you so that you can remember daily, whom he says you are and how much he adores you.

For I hold you by your right hand. I, the Lord your God. And I say to you, "Don't be afraid. I am here to help you."
(Isaiah 41:13 NLT)

_____

_____

_____

_____

_____

Chapter 27

HE'LL DO IT AGAIN

I am convinced and confident of this very thing, that
He who has begun a good work in you will [continue to]
perfect and complete it until the day of Christ Jesus [the
time of His return].

(Philippians 1:6 AMP)

For this last chapter, I want to share an amazing experience that
I had last year. I was sitting in a coffee shop in Kona, Hawaii,
during my school of counseling. As I was working hard on my
last assignment of the term, I found myself gazing at the people around
me. Suddenly, there was a flash from the Lord. He reminded me of when
I was sixteen years old and headed off for my first mission's trip. We were
going to spend two weeks in Gorlitz, Germany, working with a local
missionary who lived there. Little did I know that the trip would start a
fire for missions and a heart for Europe, which would span decades and
would grow stronger every day.

The Lord showed me a picture in my mind of the people whom I went
with and me standing in the airport in Little Rock, Arkansas, with no idea
of the journey we were about to embark on. Then the Lord softly told me
that he would renew the desires of my heart that he had birthed when I
was sixteen. Now, at that point of school and time in my life, I had no
plans to go to Germany or Europe at all. I didn't even have any contacts in
those areas. I typed up what I heard the Lord say that late afternoon and
treasured it in my heart. To be honest, I started getting a little excited, just
like that teenager in gray sweatpants and a white T-shirt who was getting
ready to fly out for her first mission's trip did. This is what I typed up to
pray into. It was what I heard him say to me that day.

Journal Entry 2021

I was sitting in a coffee shop in Kona, Hawaii, when all the sudden, I had a flashback of coming home from Germany when I was sixteen. The Lord reminded me that when I got off the plane, I was wearing this deep blue linen pants suit, which I had gotten in a department store in Gorlitz, Germany. I had left the states in sweats, but I came back in a linen pants suit. I felt the Holy Spirit say, *I'm going to take you back to those dreams and plans I had for you then, so get ready!* Oh, my goodness! Even as I write this out, I think about how my finances were covered, and I even had an abundance so that I could buy things for my family and a pants suit for myself. My mom still has the crystal goblets that I bought in Dresden. Thank you, Lord! Thank you for giving me back the years that the locust ate and even more. I get to do it with my daughter. You are restoring my dreams. Yes, I receive it in Jesus's name.

My sweet friends, I know this one thing, and I know it well. Our Lord is faithful. He is good and loving. Even when we don't see it or feel it, believe it. He will do what he says. He will show himself faithful. His promises are true, and he is faithful to complete what he starts in us.

I am so happy to tell you that I am writing the last chapter of this book in a coffee shop in Switzerland. In the morning, my daughter, a ministry friend of ours whom I met in Kona, and I are driving to Germany to minister to five hundred youths. Not only has the Lord restored the promise that he put in my heart twenty-seven years ago but I get to do it with my daughter. What an awesome God he is. I also found out that the location of the camp is only fifteen kilometers from Gorlitz, Germany, where I went when I was sixteen years old. How precise the Lord is. I rejoice over God's faithfulness.

How sweet he is to us, dear friend. Time can go by, and you feel like he's forgotten you. It was twenty-seven years from the time I went on that trip to Germany until I received this word of reassurance and the promise from the Lord. It has only been eight months since he spoke this to my spirit, and I am sitting here writing. We have to trust that his timing and ways are not ours. We believe in his goodness and trust that he is working everything out for our good and his glory. I want to share something my Grandma Rorie used to say to me. She would tell me that when I had something I was worrying and praying about, I needed to put it in the Lord's hands and not take it out. Ever since grandma told me this, I started practicing it. But recently during counseling school, I realized that there was one more step. I needed to put it in the Lord's hands and then ask for a promise or word from him to hold onto in exchange. This chapter's questions will give you a chance to try this out.

- Close your eyes and ask the Holy Spirit to show you something that he has promised you in your past. This can be any amount of time—a year, twenty-seven years, or yesterday. Write down the promise.
- Now say, "Lord, is there anything in me that causes me to doubt your word and promise?" If he brings something to mind, ask him to forgive you for believing the lie that was revealed (For example: "Forgive me for believing the lie of fear, doubt, and unworthiness…etc.).
- After asking for forgiveness, say, "Jesus, I give this to you and I ask you for a blessing or promise to replace the lie that I've been believing?" Sit and listen. He will speak something to your spirit. Write it down and now dear friend, say it out loud, over and over, day after day, until it becomes what you believe instead of the lie that the enemy has been wanting you to believe. Say something like this but with your own promises in it. *"I believe God has my back. He has my future in his hands. He will complete what he started in me. Thank you, heavenly Father.*

_____

_____

_____

_____

_____

Conclusion

I really hope you've enjoyed reading this collection of stories as much as I have enjoyed putting them together and reliving them. I want to thank all the people who allowed me to include their stories as examples of how amazing our Lord is and how we walk with Jesus through this life on Earth.

I have prayed over this book and everyone who reads it that the Lord will use these words as arms that reach out and love on each person. I pray that through this book, the Holy Spirit will blow on your life, and God will bring you his radiant peace, hope, deliverance, joy, and goodness that comes to those who love Jesus. Remember that through it all, the Lord is working all things together for the good of us who are in him. He is standing with arms opened wide and wanting to take your pain and give you a blessing in place of it, which is the great exchange.

I am including some fun stuff at the end of the book that helps me step through hard times when I get triggered and need help calming my mind, labeling the issue or attack, and then renewing my mind to receive a blessing instead. The first item is a journal entry that I felt the Lord gave me back in 2017. I'm adding this because I feel like it is time to release it. The second item is what I'm calling, "The Great Exchange Experience." This will step you through a trigger and help you renew your mind. The third item is some of my personal experiences of spending time with Jesus.

From My Journal Entry in 2017

I feel the Lord is whispering to me, *I want my people to know why they are Christ Followers, so they will be able to stand strong. The only way to endure is falling in love with me. They have to know what they were created for and why. I will pour out my Spirit on them, and they will know what to do and when to do it. Don't be discouraged or dismayed. Only know me.*

What else do I have to tell you? You were created for such a time as this. Why else would I warn you and speak to you? You are mine, and I love you. I have always loved you with everlasting love. I am the God who created you, and you have a purpose and calling. Why are you waiting? Why? Do you think my blood is not sufficient? Why do you run and hide as Adam did? I am your all in all, and I redeem you. You have been redeemed. You have been assigned. You have been equipped. Reach down deep and know that I can do all things through you. You only need to surrender to me. You only need me. You are my only, and I am yours. Let my Holy God Spirit ignite you. Your embers have been low, but I am ready to stir them up. I do it now. I need your particular part in this last great outpouring. Oh, how I love you, dear warrior. You feel lowly in spirit and useless, but I say you are a Mighty Warrior, and what I say is what is! Now is the time My Banner is Raised …

Put on your armor and run out to fight.

If I am for you, who can be against you?

Know who you fight for and be equipped to do My will.

Rest at night and wake up energized with God energy.

I will wash your armor as you sleep, and I will replenish you as you rest.

I will have your daily portion ready when you rise.

Then I will help you dress for your day so that you are ready to go out and confront the enemy's lines.

Do not look to the left or the right, focus on the unseen and not the seen.

My watchmen are on the walls announcing the time.

Do not be asleep. Be actively in faith and awaiting my call.

The Great Exchange Experience

W rite down your response to the questions below in the space provided. As you do so, it will help you process through your triggers and issues and allow a place for the Lord to give you healing in these areas as well as blessings to believe and declare. Follow up on the next page with how to walk through receiving your new declarations and declaring them.

Issue	Mind	Action
What is the need or trigger you are dealing with today?	What are your thoughts and feelings associated with this issue?	As a result of this issue, how did you behave or how are you behaving currently?

Fill out the questions below honestly. As you do so, it will help you process through your traumas and issues and allow a place for the Lord to give you healing in these areas as well as blessings to believe and declare.

Healing Steps

Say Aloud to the Lord in Prayer and Declaration:

1. Lord, I confess my sins relating to this issue.
   List anything that came up when you listed your feelings, thoughts, and behaviors in the above section that go against the Word and promises of God.

2. I forgive those who contributed to this issue, knowingly or unknowingly, and I forgive myself.
   I forgive my mother, etc. The Bible tells us, "Death and life are in the power of the tongue" (Proverbs 18:21 AMP), so listing each person you need to forgive releases you from the hold that unforgiveness has in your life.

3. Holy Spirit, what blessing(s) do you want to give me in place of the issue I've been dealing with?

Close your eyes and let the Holy Spirit speak to your spirit and give you the blessing that he wants you to Believe, Receive, and Declare every time the issue comes to mind.

After receiving your blessing(s) from the Lord, you can put it on your mirror, on your phone alerts, in your car, or anywhere you will see these promises every day until they become second nature to you and what you believe deep down. You can do these healing steps as many times as you need to and for as many issues as you need to have healing in.

Blessings in Jesus's name, my dear friend!

Stepping Behind the Veil

I use this process when I need a big breakthrough and word from the Lord. You don't have to do this every day or the same way that I do it. I like to learn the different ways others do their quiet time with the Lord. I thought I would put this in at the end. I pray that the personal application questions at the end of most chapters have been a blessing to you. It has really been a blessing to me to slow down, close my eyes, still my mind and spirit, and interact with Jesus. My hope is that you also have benefited from this exercise. It allows you to learn how to be still and know that he is God, anywhere and at any time, even when a prayer closet isn't handy. Thank you again for reading this book and letting me share my heart and journey with you. Many blessings to you, my dear friend.

This is what I do. You can follow it as much as you feel led.

- I wake up, get a cup of coffee or tea, and go to a private area to spend time with the Lord. This can be a closet, the living room (which is where I do mine before anyone else gets up), or even your car. Just find a place where you can be alone with Jesus and feel free to talk out loud if you want. I remember hearing stories about my great-grandma going behind their stove and crying out to the Lord after breakfast every day. You might have to try a few places until you find a good fit.

- Then I turn on instrumental worship music to create a worship atmosphere. I have personally found that worship music with words sidetracks me. I'm about to enter the presence of the Lord, and I want to clearly hear what he is saying, but you find what works best for you. I also grab a notebook to jot down anything the Holy Spirit reveals to me while we are spending time together.

~ Something I started doing about three years ago was kneeling down. I was at my great aunt Marie's house (She is ninety-eight). She told me that one morning when she was trying to get up from her knees after she had been in prayer, she couldn't get up. She said that her body locked up. She ended up being there for a few hours. *Oh, my!* I thought. *Lord, I'm so sorry for not honoring you more in the simple things.* My great aunt wasn't going to miss crying out to her Lord just because it was hard to get up. I have found that this act of surrender submits my sore back, rushed pace, and desires and lays them at his feet.

~ Then I start worshiping, thanking, and praising the Lord and praying in my prayer language. I imagine that I have stepped into the opening in the veil. I step over and enter the holy place. The smoke from the incense is all around. His throne glows in the center of the room, and it is elevated above everything else. I make my way up the golden stairs to where Jesus sits at the right hand of our Father—our Abba, which means Daddy. He is our almighty, holy, heavenly Daddy, God. Jesus reaches out his arms for me to climb into his lap like a child. I sit there with Jesus in Heavenly places and turn to the Father to gauge his heart and mood. I always get lost in the never-ending pools of love in his eyes. I can't help but tell him how incredible he is and that he is my God, the one and only God, the lover of my soul, my best friend, and the Lord of my life.

~ After I have loved on the Lord for a while, I say the Lord's Prayer, not in a legalistic way but as an outline. I say something like, *Heavenly Father, you are so holy, and your name is hallowed. You are the only God, and you're my God. I lay my life down at your feet. Your Kingdom come, and your will be done on earth as it is in heaven. Your kingdom come, and your will be done in my life and my family and friends' lives* [I list them], *as it is in heaven. I want to walk in your will, heavenly Father. Give me what I need for today—real bread but most importantly, your word concerning my life for today. What I need for life today is a word from you for me to hold onto.*

Forgive me of my sins as I forgive those who sin against me. Holy Spirit, show me anyone whom I have not forgiven or hold something against. Bring it to my mind so that I can walk in forgiveness before you. Lead me not into temptation and deliver me from evil. Guard my coming and going and bless my day. For thine is the kingdom, the glory, and the power that I live for, I walk in, and what I have available to me in the authority of Jesus's name.

Next, I say something like, *Lord, what do you want to say to me today? I'm listening, Holy Spirit. Quiet my heart, clear my mind, and give me the mind of Christ. I reject any voice of the enemy through the authority of Jesus Christ.*

Then I sit still, breathe deeply, and listen. When I say listen, I don't mean that you will hear a Charlton Heston deep voice coming from the great beyond. You might hear a still, small voice. You might have a thought that gives you chills because it comes from the Spirit with power. Sometimes the Lord will drop a picture into your mind, or a scene will play out in your head. It could be an unexplainable peace and alignment with him to start your day. You will know how long to sit in his presence. Whatever he gives you or causes you to feel, just pray into that. *Lord, keep this with me all day during whatever I face. I'm yours, and you are in control.*

Remember what my Grandma Rorie used to say: "Put it in the Lord's hands and don't take it back out." Give it all to him and walk into your day with peace. Be equipped with every spiritual weapon you need for the day. Remember, our battle is not against flesh and blood, but against the rulers, authorities, world powers of darkness, and spiritual forces of evil in the heavens. We walk in the assurance that it's not by might nor by power but by the Holy Spirit that we live and move and have our being. We walk in alignment with Jesus and in his peace. We will carry it out into the world. The children of Israel would only gather enough manna and quail that they needed for that day; otherwise, it would go bad. Daily, we get up, go behind the veil, and get our provision for the day. He has prepared so much for us. Before we know it, we will find ourselves saying, "You just can't make this stuff up!"

Be blessed, dear friend

Mary Brooks

Printed in the United States
by Baker & Taylor Publisher Services